これだけできるようにがんばろう。

1 友だちを5ついじょうの文を使ってしょうかいできます。
Able to introduce my friends using five sentences or more.

2 5か国語であいさつができます。
Able to greet in five different languages.

3 今、何をしているかを、動作をつけながら言うことができます。
Able to gesture and say what I am doing.

4 起きる時間と、ねる時間を言うことができます。
Able to say what time I get up and go to bed.

5 好きな科目を言うことができます。
Able to say what subject I like.

6 今日の日付と天気を言うことができます。
Able to say today's date and weather.

7 自分のたん生日を言うことができ、お友だちのたん生日を聞くことができます。
Able to say when my birthday is and ask my friends theirs.

8 友だち3人の好きなスポーツを言うことができます。
Able to say three of my friends' favorite sports.

9 1日ですることを5ついじょう言えます。
Able to say five things I do in a day.

10 テキストの中の を10こいじょう言うことができます。
Able to recite ten chants from the CHANTS pages. 8 10 12 20 24 26 30 32 34 36 38 40 42 44 48 52 54 56

11 テキストの中の を6ついじょう言うことができます。
Able to say six dialogs and/or speeches in the textbook. 4 6 14 16 18 22 28 46 50 62

12 テキストの中の を3つ歌うことができます。
Able to sing three songs from the SONG pages. 5 7 27 35 53 55 58

13 テキストの中の を1つ大きな声で発表することができます。
Able to recite one story from the textbook in a loud voice. 58 60

14 先生が見せるthree-letter wordsを10個、ストーリーを1つ読むことができます。
Able to read ten three-letter words and one story my teacher shows me correctly. 27 39

15 先生が見せるカードを10個正しく読むことができます。
Able to read ten words/ expressions my teacher shows me correctly.

16 テキストの左ページの英語をノートに全ページ書き写しました。
Copied all the pages of English on the left page of the text into my notebook.

17 自分のことを6つ以上の文を使ってはっきり言うことができます。
Able to give a speech about myself clearly using in 6 or more sentences.

○の中の数字(すうじ)はページをあらわしています。

3→4

Hello! My name is Mark. My family name is Cates.
I live in Vancouver, Canada. I'm eight years old.
This is my friend, Yumi. Her family name is Suzuki.
She is from Kobe, Japan. She is eight years old, too.

5

a b c d e f g h i

j k l m n o p q r

s t u v w x y z

A to Z

2

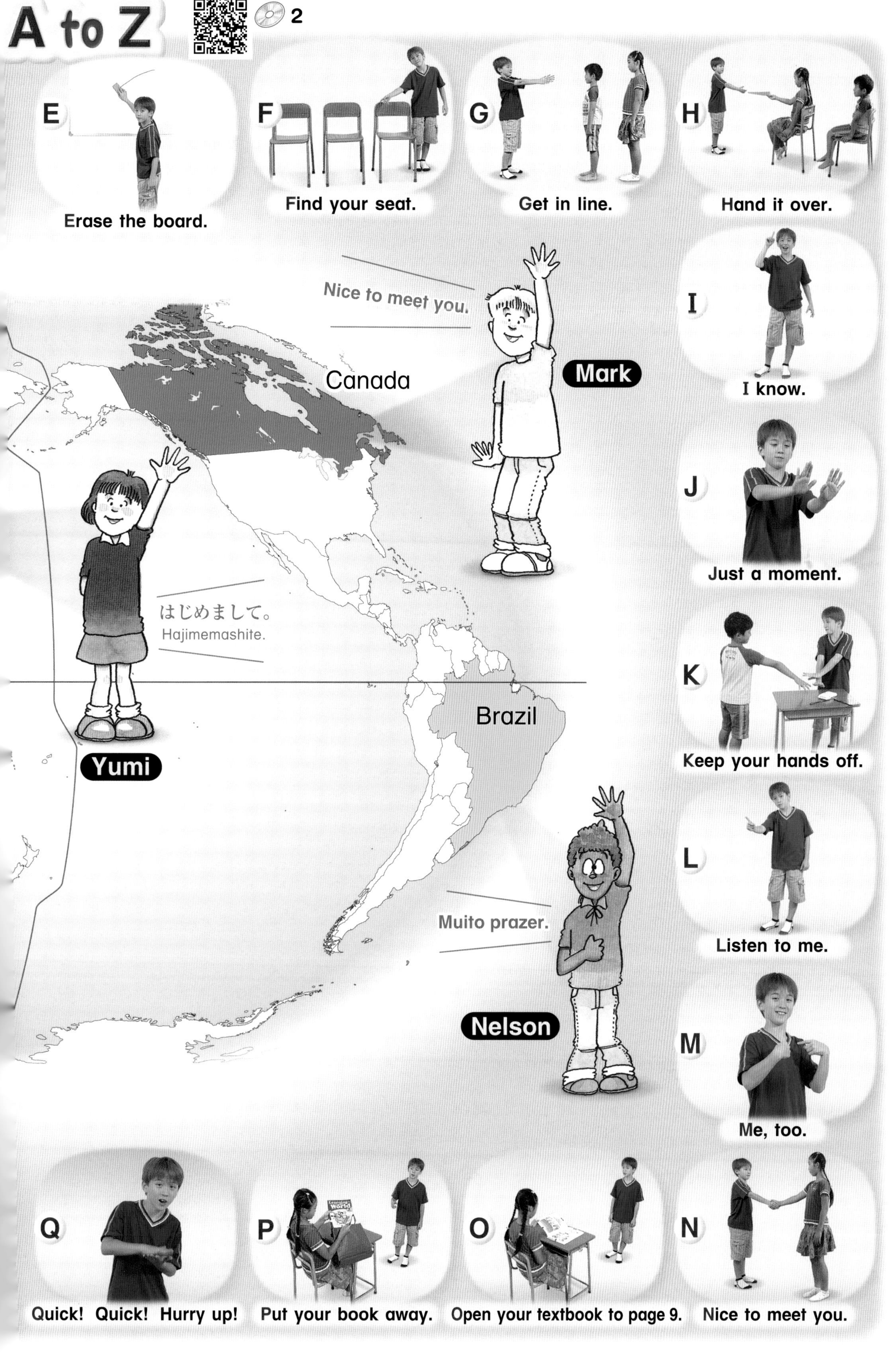

E
Erase the board.
F
Find your seat.
G
Get in line.
H
Hand it over.
Nice to meet you.
Mark
Canada
I
I know.
J
Just a moment.
はじめまして。
Hajimemashite.
Yumi
Brazil
K
Keep your hands off.
L
Listen to me.
Muito prazer.
Nelson
M
Me, too.
Q
Quick! Quick! Hurry up!
P
Put your book away.
O
Open your textbook to page 9.
N
Nice to meet you.

CONTENTS

WELCOME
World
PINK
WELCOME
World
WELCOME
World
Learning World 1
READY
World
Learning World 2
Learning World 3
Learning World 4 BRIDGE
Learning World 5 TOMORROW

Learning World 2

STUDENT BOOK

Mikiko Nakamoto

with

Let's communicate in English!

ラーニングワールドシリーズは9巻から成り、幼児～小学高学年までそれぞれの発達段階に応じて書かれています。本シリーズはヒューマニスティック・アプローチとコミュニカティブ・アプローチを取り入れ、従来の、暗記とパターンプラクティス中心の英語教育ではなく、「答えが1つでない」英語による言語教育を目指しています。子供達の発話に重要な「自分の意見の構築」「自尊心の育成」「他者への許容」等が英語の四技能の学習を通して習得できるようにしています。また、子供達の日常生活に合った楽しいチャンツ、歌、会話で目標文が無理なく効果的に定着できます。テキストは10ユニットあり、各レッスンにインフォメーション・ギャップのあるコミュニケーション活動を紹介しています。本テキストでは「到達度評価のためのAchievement Targets (p.3)」を活用し年度末の1か月をかけて総復習を行い、17の課題を達成することを目指します。3rd Editionでは音声とチャンツ動画のQRコードを付し、各右ページで使う語彙や英文の音声を追加しました。

このテキストには、次のマークが入っています。なにをするのか、見てわかるようになりましょう。

Words

たんごをおぼえましょう。

Communication activity

英語を使って、おともだちや先生と
協力して、かつどうしましょう。

Dialog

会話文をおぼえましょう。

Oral Presentation

自分のかんがえを、みんなのまえで
はっぴょうしましょう。

Chant

リズムにのっておぼえましょう。

Exercise

問題をときましょう。

Speech

スピーチをおぼえましょう。

Song

げんきよく歌いましょう。

Story

ストーリーをおぼえましょう。

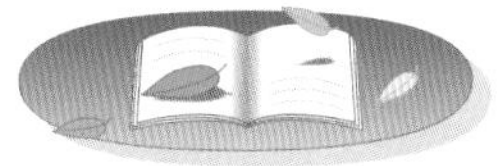

Phonics

読んでみましょう。

Interview Game

おともだちや先生に質問しましょう。

Listening Test

英語を聞いて答えましょう。
どれだけ聞きとれるかな？

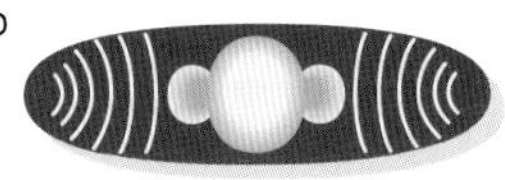

おうちで音声を聞きましょう。  **3→4**

チャンツ動画を楽しく活用しましょう。 

Communication activity

128

- Hello. What is your name?
- My name is Terry.
- How do you spell Terry?
- T, E, R, R, Y. Terry.

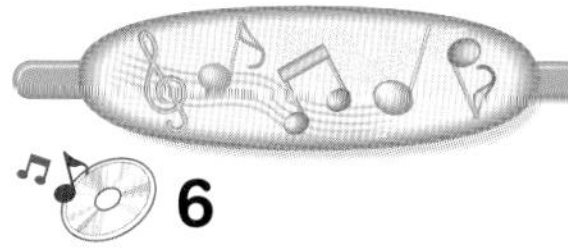

6

Me Myself

My name is Mark. My family name is Cates.
I live in Vancouver. I'm eight years old now.
Hello. Hello. Hello, hello my friend. Hello. Hello. Hello, my friend.

Hello.

My name is ______________________ .

I live in ______________________ ,

______________________ .

Nice to meet you.

Alphabet train

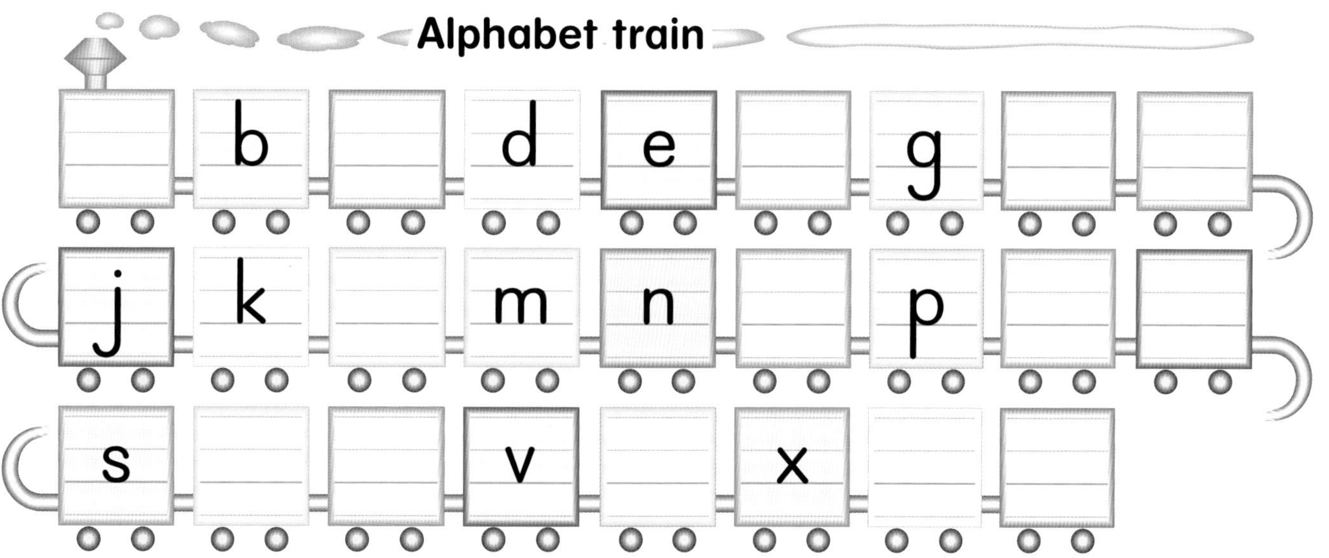

My name is Mark.
I'm from Canada.
Nice to meet you.

My name is Yumi.
I'm from Japan.
Hajimemashite.
はじめまして。

My name is Min.
I'm from Korea.
Cho-um poep-ke-sum-ni-da.
처음 뵙겠습니다.

My name is Nelson.
I'm from Brazil.
Muito prazer.

My name is Ema.
I'm from France.
Enchantée.

Words

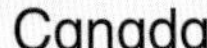
Canada

Japan

Korea

Brazil

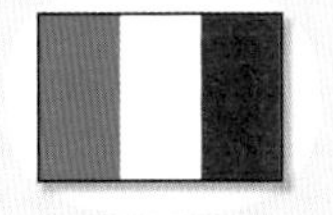
France

Communication activity

- I am from Korea.
- This is the flag of Korea.

  Cho-um poep-ke-sum-ni-da.

129

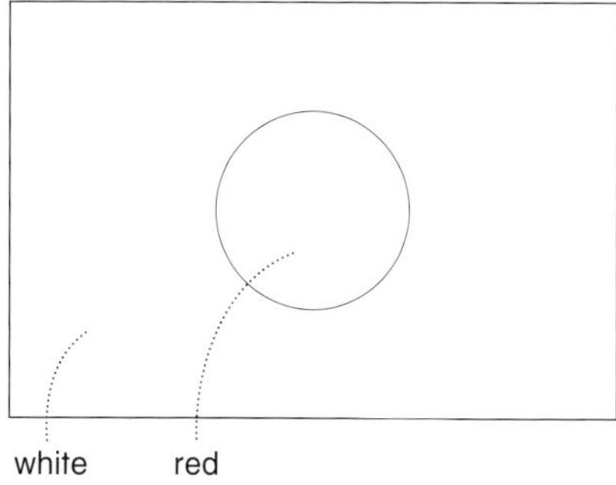

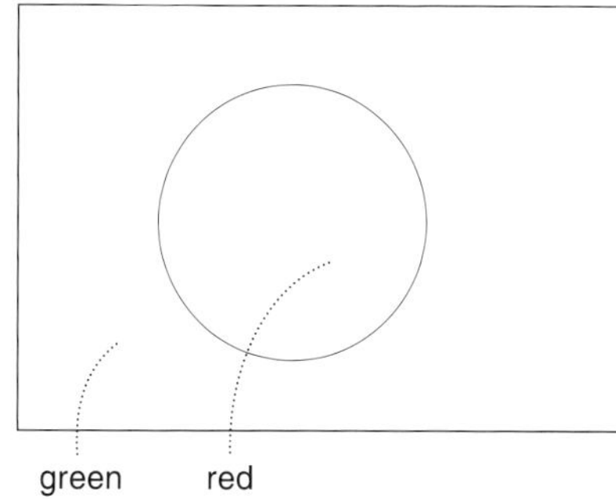

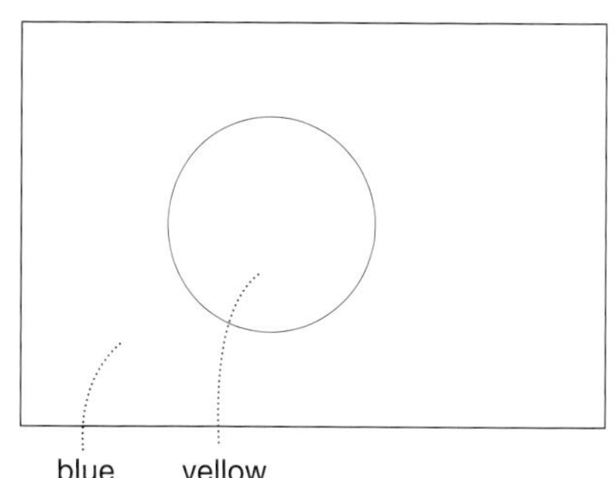

 10

Hello Song

Hello.

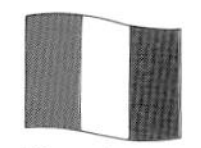
Bonjour.

Ni hao.

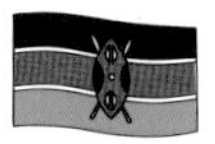

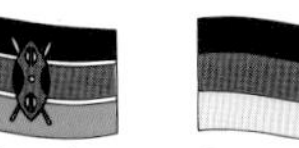
Hujambo.

Guten Tag.

Buenos dias.

Annyeong hasimnikka.

Sawas dee.

Namaste.

Konnichiwa.

1

a 

b 

c 

2

a 

b 

c 

3

a 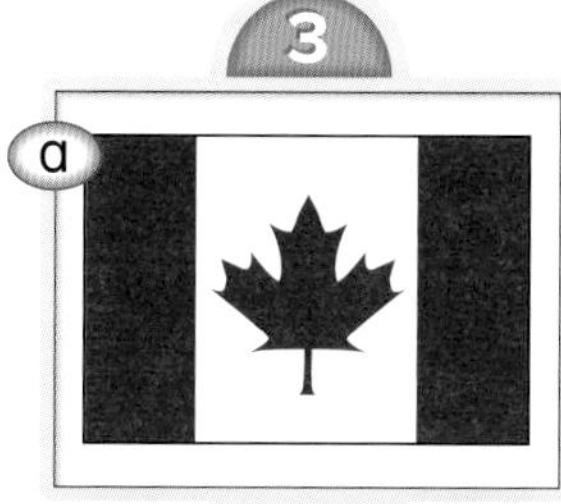

b 

c 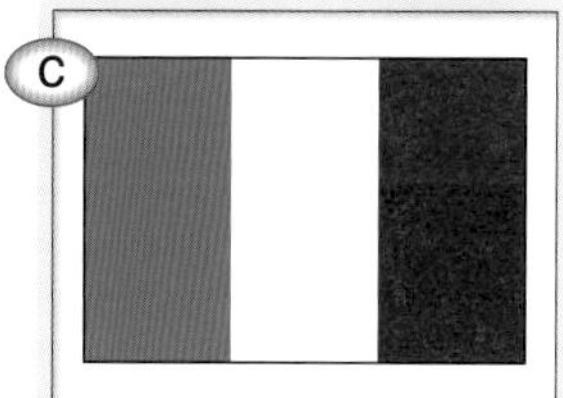

4

a 

b 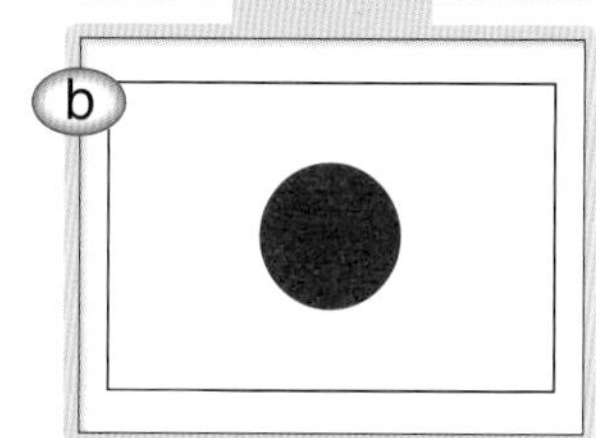

c 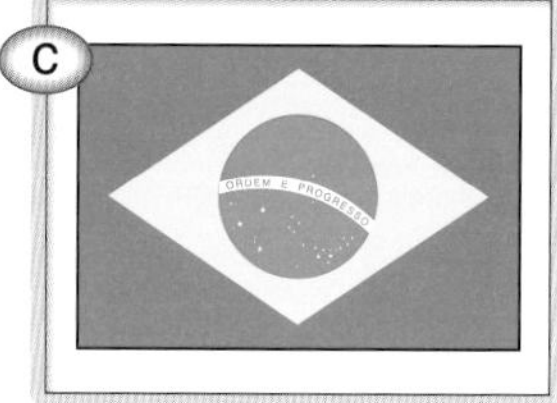

What's his name?

His name is Mark.

What's her name?

Her name is Yumi.

What's her name?

Her name is Min.

What's her name?

Her name is Ema.

What's his name?

His name is Nelson.

Nelson

Communication activity

130

- What's his name?
- His name is Terry.
- What's her name?
- Her name is Yuka.

This is my friend.

His / Her name is ______________________

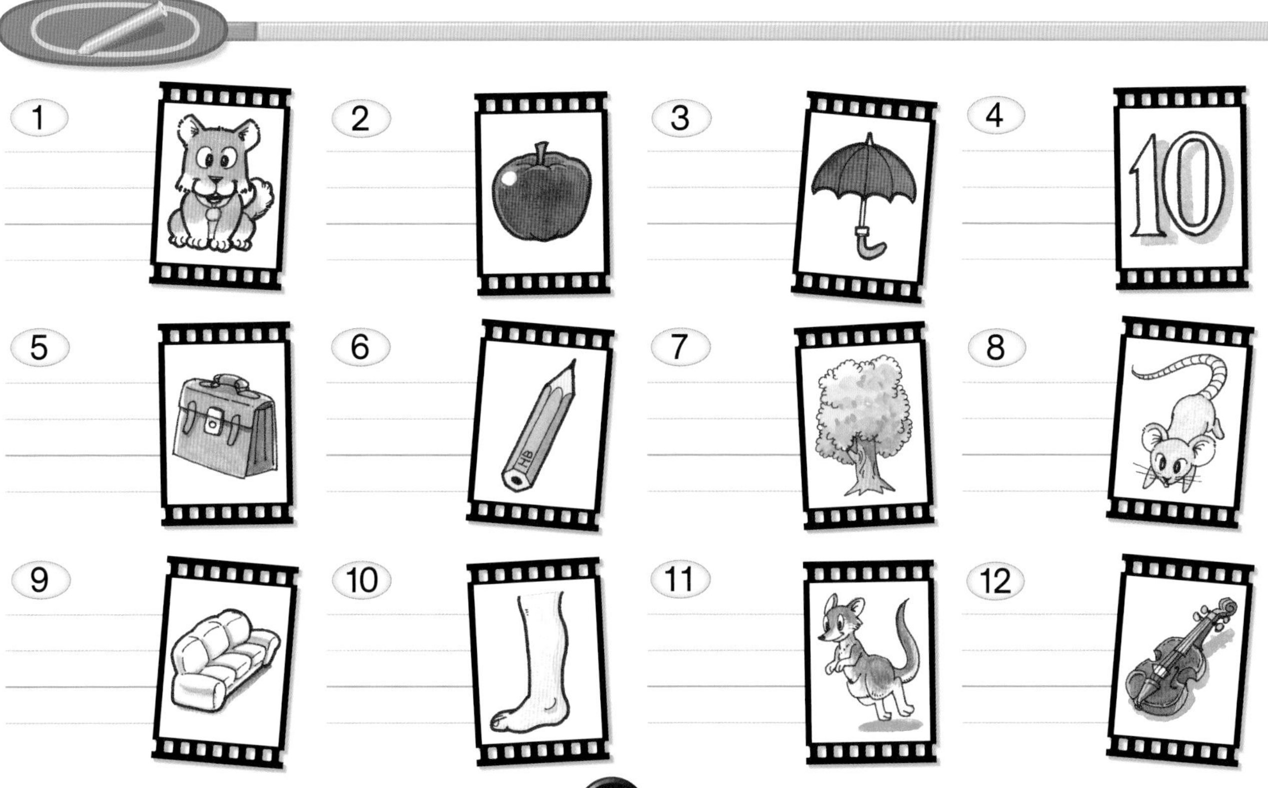

13 → 14

I am walking.
You are walking.
He is walking.
She is walking.

WE ARE WALKING ON THE EARTH!

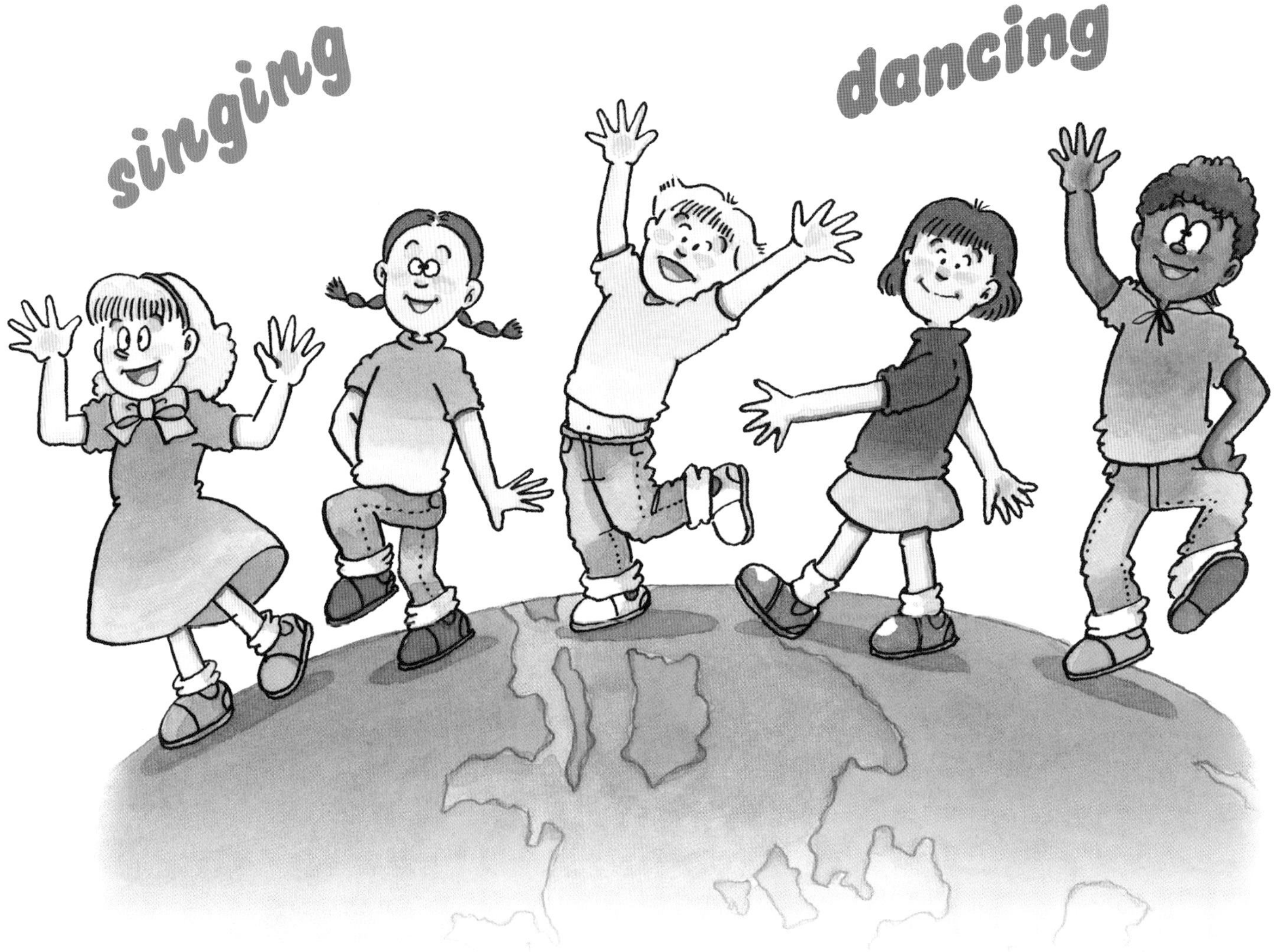

singing

dancing

15

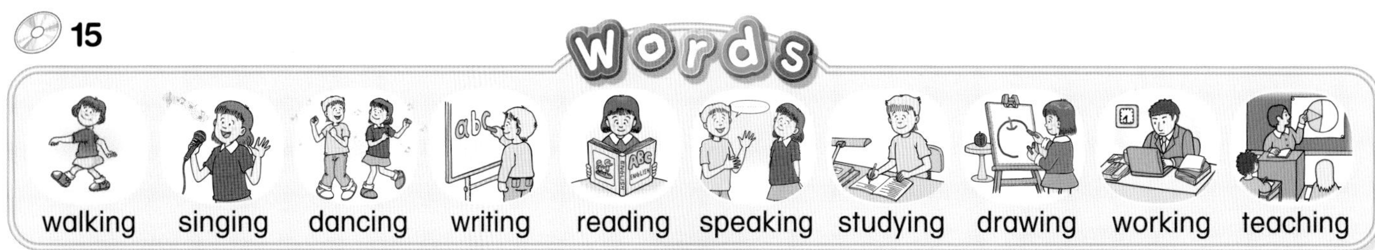

Communication activity

◉)131

- What am I doing?
- You are singing.

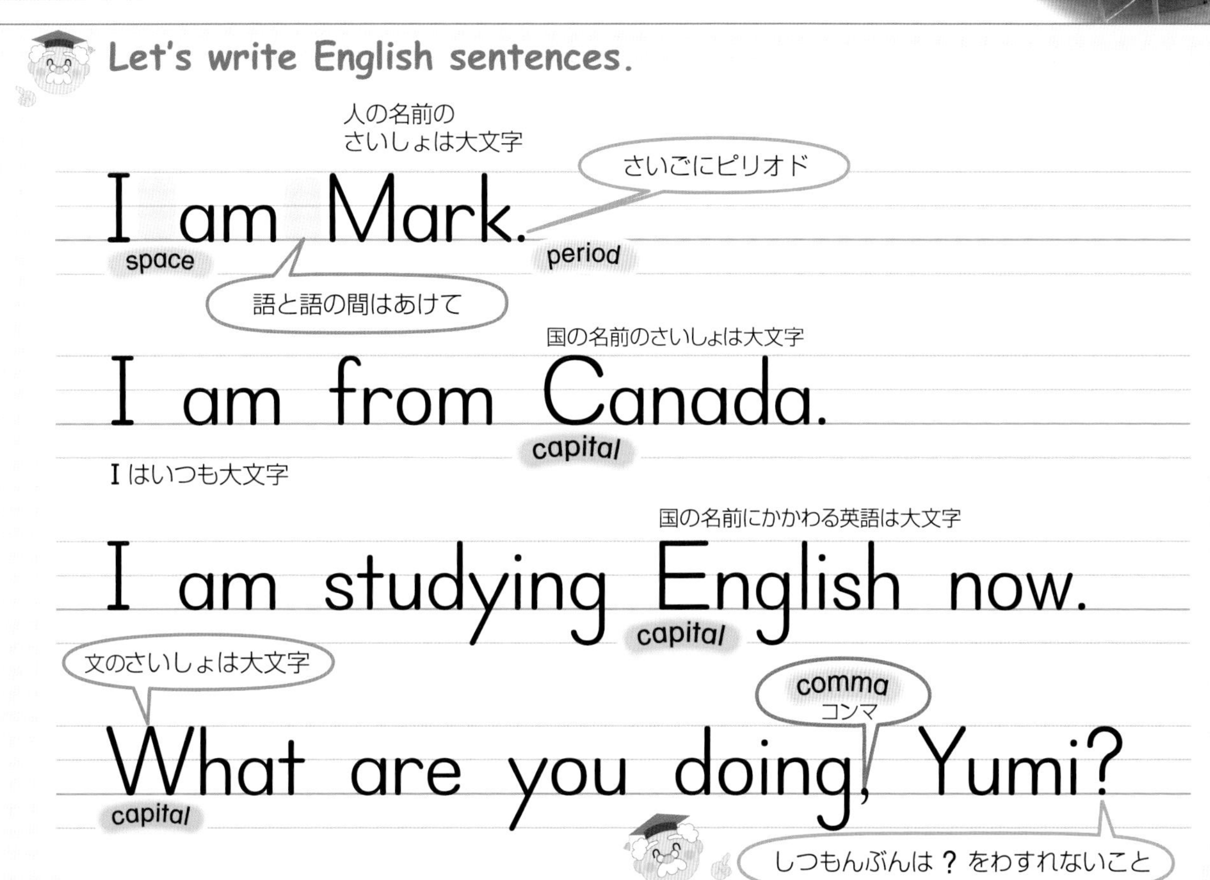

16→17

How's Mark?

He is sleepy.
He's always sleepy.

How's Nelson?

He is hungry.
He's always hungry.

How's Yumi?

She is fine.
She's always fine.

How's Min?

She is tired.
She's always tired.

How's Ema?

She is angry.
She's always angry.

I am happy. You are happy. They are happy. We are happy.

How is = How's
He is = He's
She is = She's

18

Words

sleepy

fine

hungry

tired

angry

happy

sad

sick

full

thirsty

Communication activity

🔊132

- Is Mark sleepy?
- Yes, he is.
  No, he isn't.

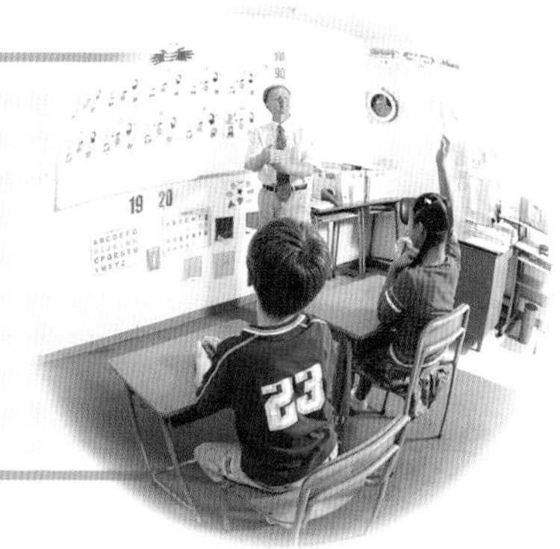

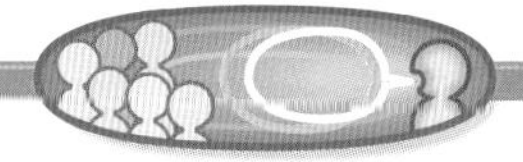

I am ______________ today.

______________ is ______________ today.

1

a 

b 

c 

2

a 

b 

c 

3

a 

b 

c 

4

a 

b 

c 

19 → 20

Which is your kite? Is it a rectangle?

No, it isn't. It's a triangle.

Is it big?

No, it isn't.

Is it red?

Yes, it is.

A little red triangle...
Oh, that's your kite, Min.

21

Words

rectangle triangle circle square star crescent diamond heart oval

Communication activity

133

- Which is your kite?
- Is it a triangle?
- Yes, it is. / No, it isn't.
- It is a big blue triangle.

My kite

Is it big?

Is it a triangle?

What color is it?

It's a

Which is your kite?

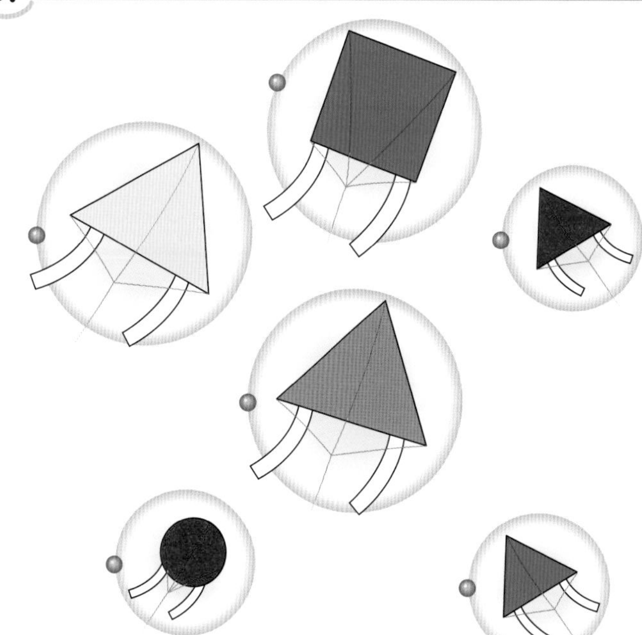

22→23

It's six thirty.
Time to wake up.

wake up

It's seven fifty.
Time to go to school.

go to school

It's three fifteen.
Time to go home.

go home

It's eight o'clock.
Time to do your homework.

do (your) homework

It's nine twenty.
Time to take a bath.

take a bath

It's nine forty-five.
Time to go to bed.

go to bed

24

Words

0	1	2	3	4	5	6	7	8	9	10	11	12	13	14	15	16	17	18	19	20
zero	one	two	three	four	five	six	seven	eight	nine	ten	eleven	twelve	thirteen	fourteen	fifteen	sixteen	seventeen	eighteen	nineteen	twenty
21	22	23	24	25	26	27	28	29	30	31	32	33	34	35	36	37	38	39	40
									thirty										forty
41	42	43	44	45	46	47	48	49	50	51	52	53	54	55	56	57	58	59	60
									fifty										sixty

Communication activity

🔊134

- How do you go from one to thirty?
- I go from one, to five, to six..., then thirty.

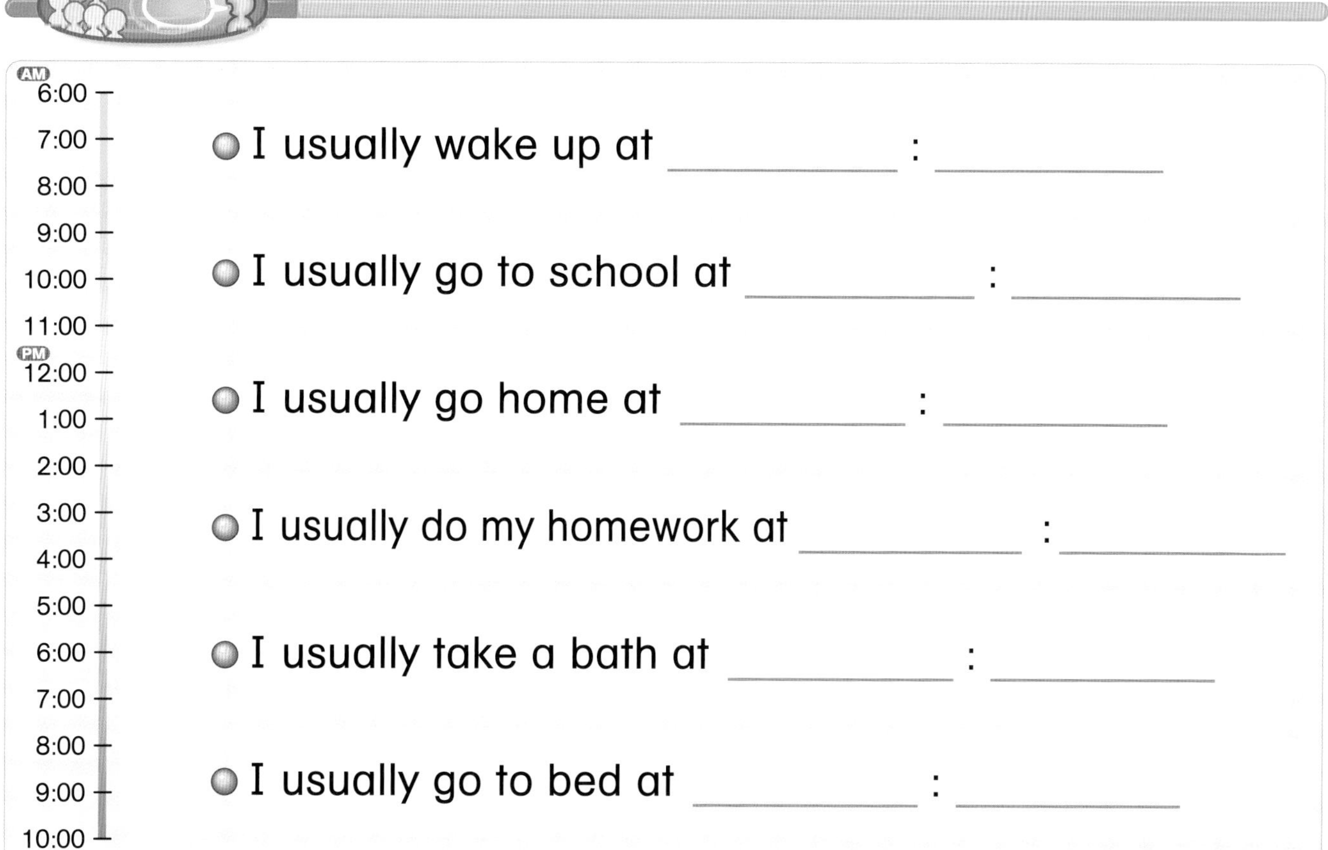

- I usually wake up at ________ : ________
- I usually go to school at ________ : ________
- I usually go home at ________ : ________
- I usually do my homework at ________ : ________
- I usually take a bath at ________ : ________
- I usually go to bed at ________ : ________

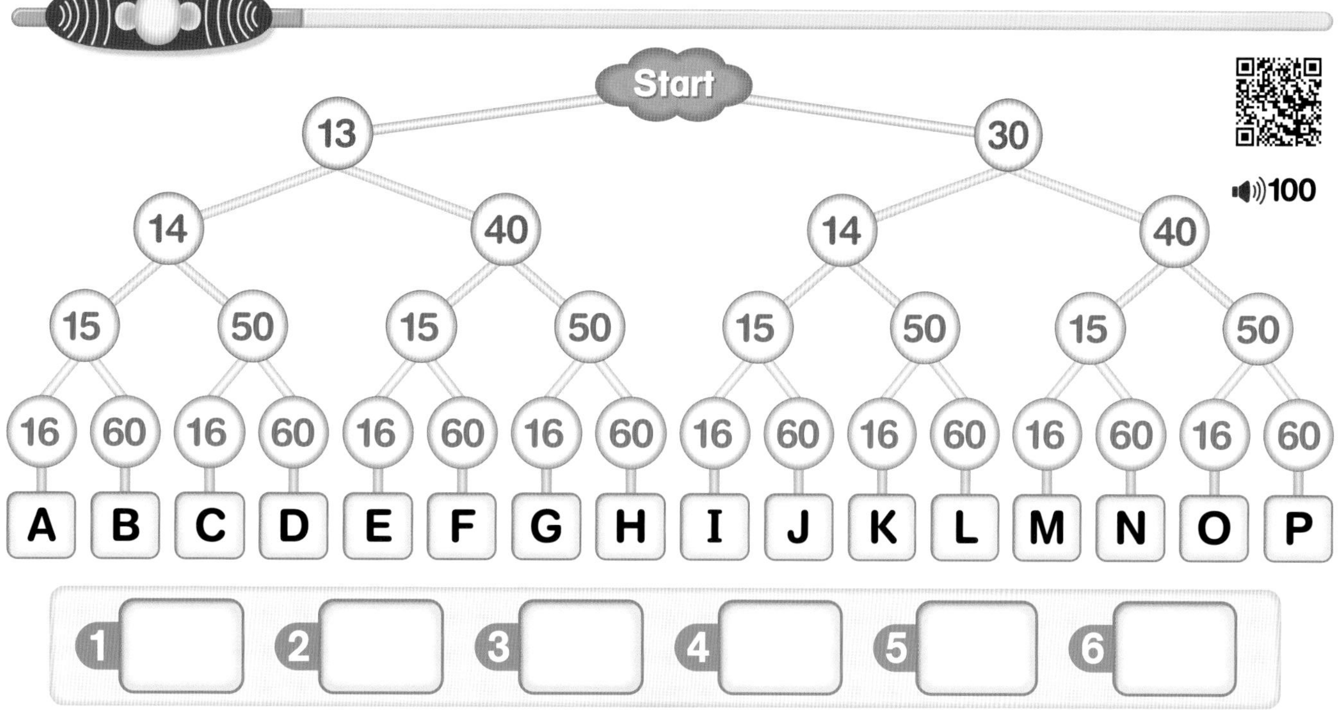

25→26

 Can I have an ice cream cone, please?

 Which size do you want?

 Triple, please.

 I want mint, vanilla and chocolate.

 Here you are.

 Thank you.

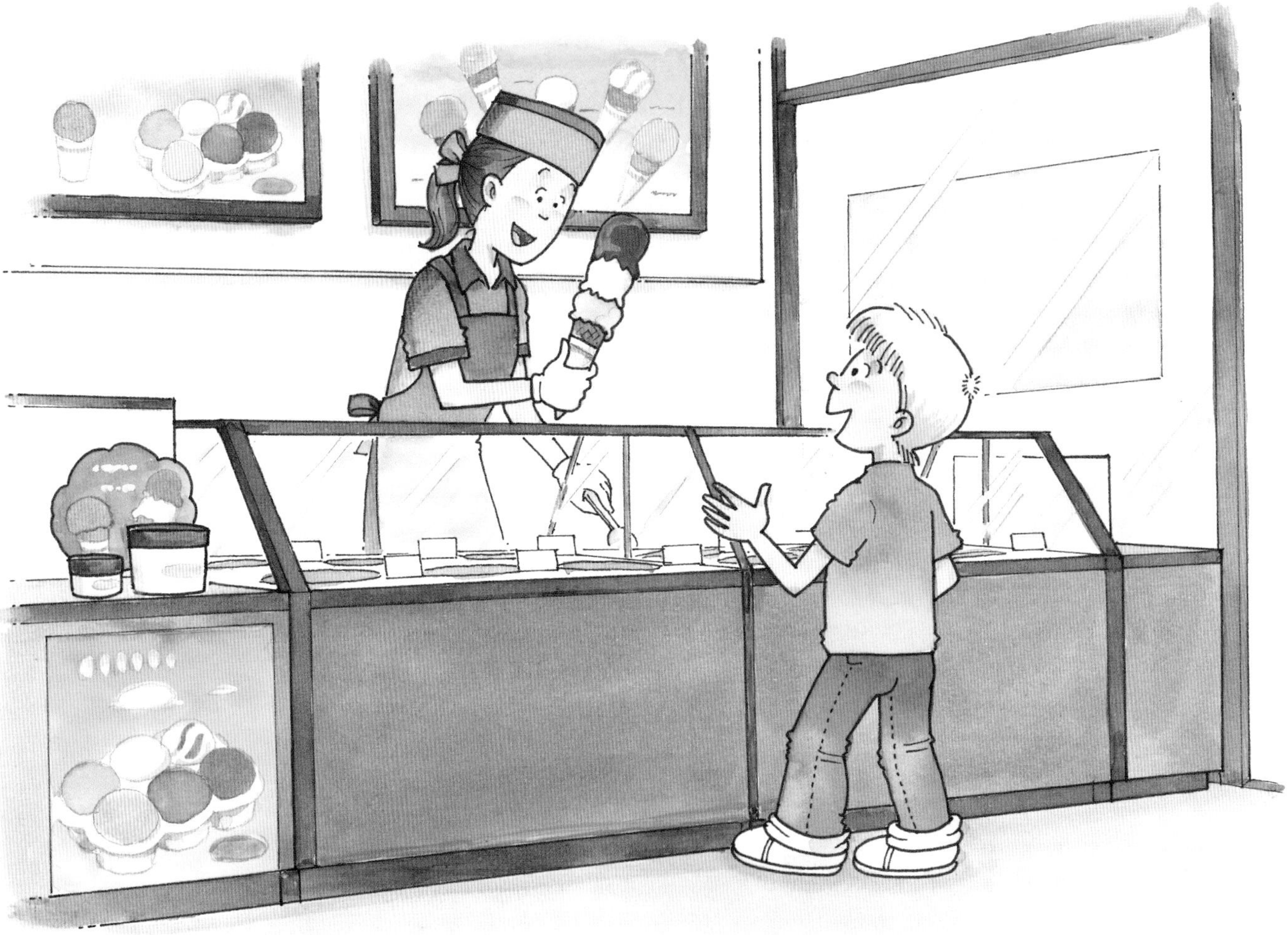

27

Communication activity

🔊135

- Which ice cream cone do you want?
- I want a triple with mint, vanilla and chocolate.

My ice cream cone

I want

______________________ ,

______________________ ,

and

______________________ .

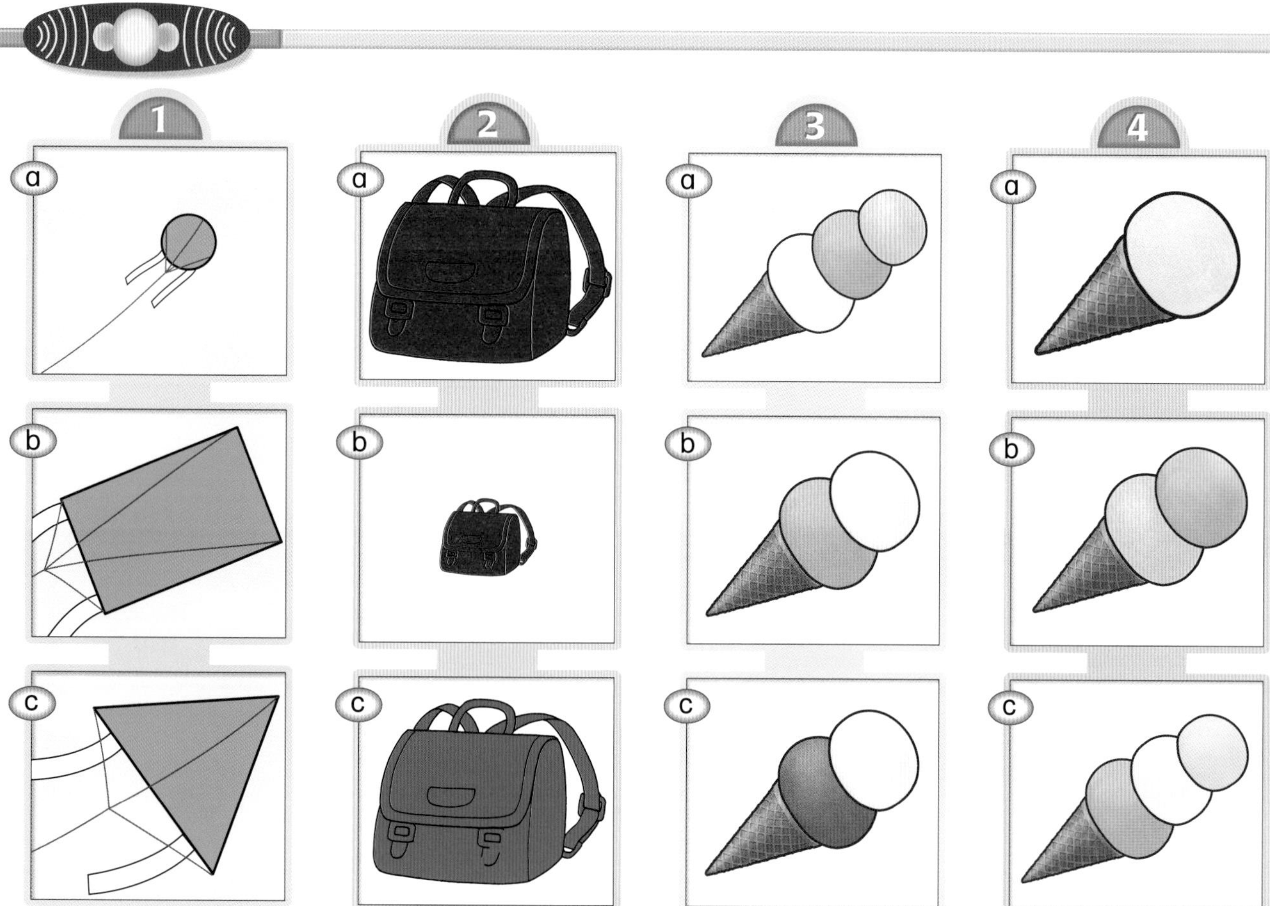

What's that?

cat

hat

bat

jet

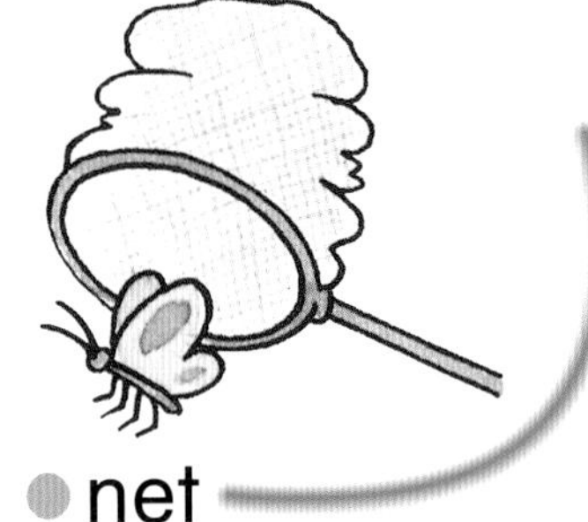

net

pet

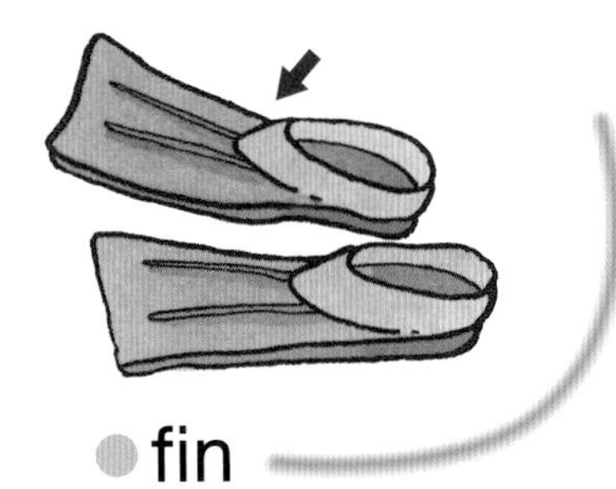

fin

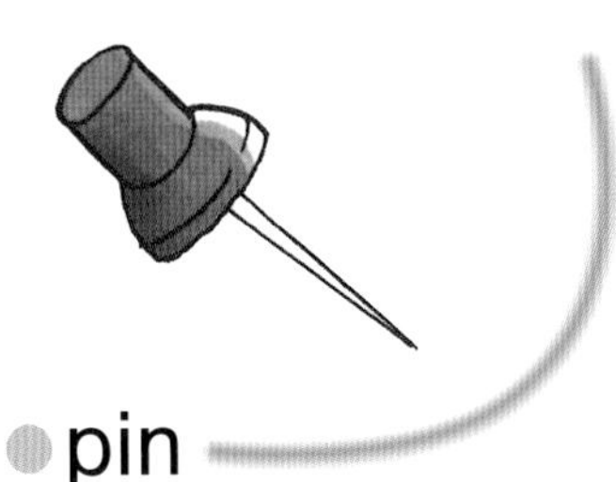

pin

chin

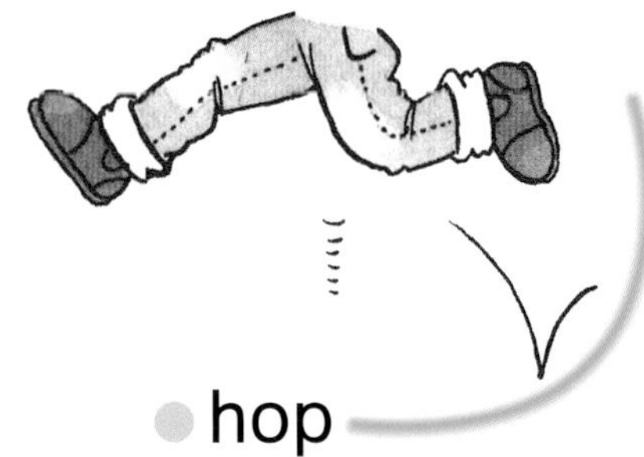

hop

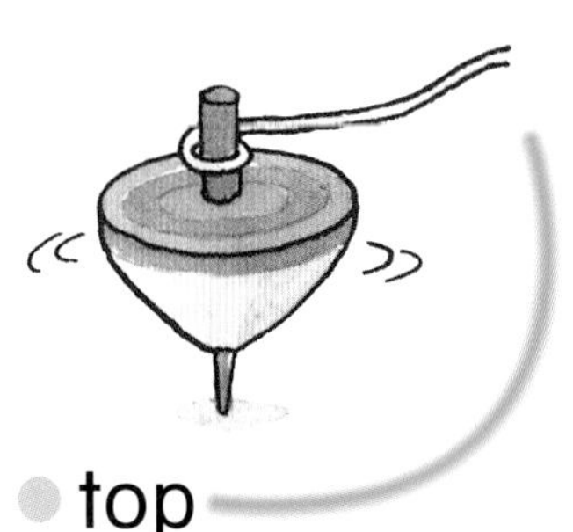

top

mop

sun

bun

gun

Communication activity

🔊136

- Let's make three-letter words.
- 'b'—'a'—'t', 'b'-'a'-'t', 'b' 'a' 't', 'bat'.

Let's read.

🔊101

a	at	pat	rat	sat	mat	fat
e	et	wet	vet	met	pet	get
i	it	bit	fit	hit	mit	sit
o	ot	cot	dot	hot	lot	not
u	ut	cut	nut	but	gut	hut

Three-letter words train

 What do you have today?

 I have math, English, science and P.E.

 Do you like math?

 No, I don't. Do you?

 Yes, I do.

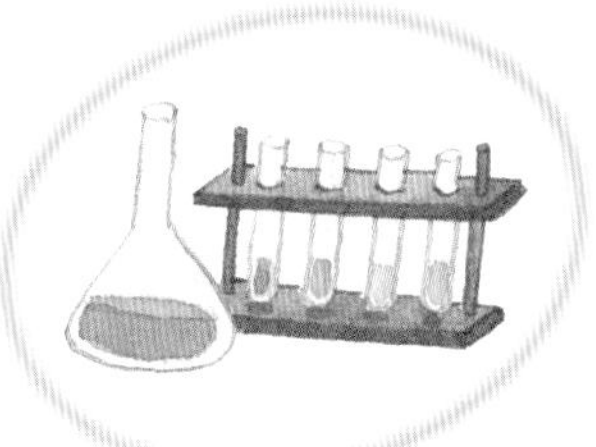

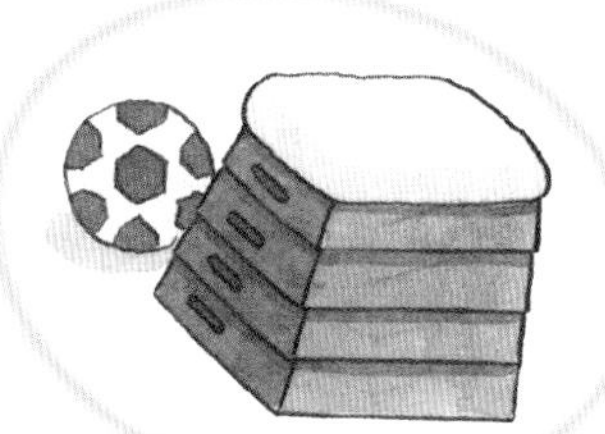

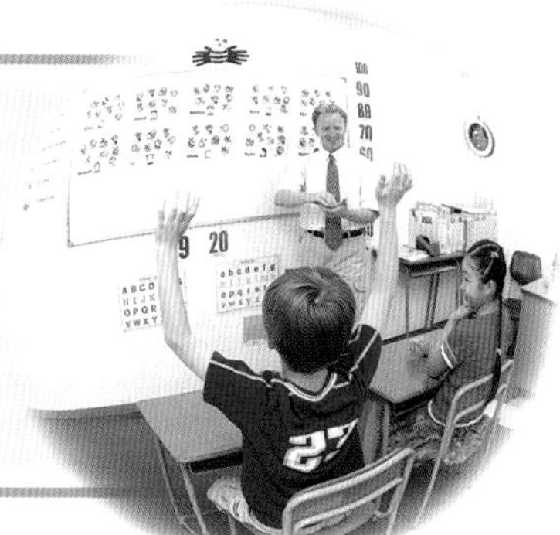

🔊137

- Guess who I am.
- Do you like math?
- Yes, I do. / No, I don't.

1. Do you like math? Yes, I do. / No, I don't.
2. Do you like social studies?
3. Do you like science?
4. Do you like music?
5. Do you like P.E.?
6. Do you like English?
7. Do you like Japanese?

Do you have a dog?
No, I don't.
Do you want a dog?
Yes, I do.
I want a big black dog.

Do you have a cat?
No, I don't.
Do you want a cat?
Yes, I do.
I want a little white cat.

35

Words

Communication activity

138

- Let's make a nice dog.
- Do you want a short tail or a long tail for your dog?
- I want a short tail.

I want a ________ dog with a ________ head,

________ ears, ________ legs and a ________ tail.

little big short long

36→37

Do you have a map or mop?
I have a map, m, a, p, map.

Do you have a nut or net?
I have a net, n, e, t, net.

Do you have a pen or pin?
I have a pin, p, i, n, pin.

Do you have a pet or pot?
I have a pot, p, o, t, pot.

Do you have a cup or cap?
I have a cup, c, u, p, cup.

a
e
i
o
u

38

map
cap
cup
pen
pin
mop
nut
net
fin
pot
pet
jet

Communication activity

139

- What is in box No.1?
- I know! C, a, p, cap.

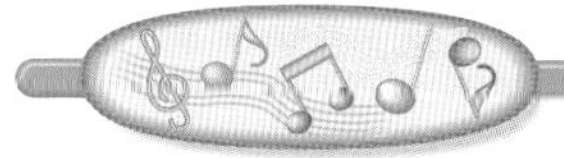

39

Little a, little a, [æ] [æ] [æ], *little a, little a,* [æ] [æ] [æ],
Tell me words with *a* *in the middle, bat, cap, cat, fan, hat.*
Little e, little e, [e] [e] [e], *little e, little e,* [e] [e] [e],
Tell me words with *e* *in the middle, bed, hen, jet, net, pen.*
Little i, little i, [i] [i] [i], *little i, little i,* [i] [i] [i],
Tell me words with *i* *in the middle, fin, lip, pig, pin, six.*
Little o, little o, [ɔ] [ɔ] [ɔ], *little o, little o,* [ɔ] [ɔ] [ɔ],
Tell me words with *o* *in the middle, box, dog, fox, hop, mop.*
Little u, little u, [ʌ] [ʌ] [ʌ], *little u, little u,* [ʌ] [ʌ] [ʌ],
Tell me words with *u* *in the middle, bug, bun, bus, cup, gun.*

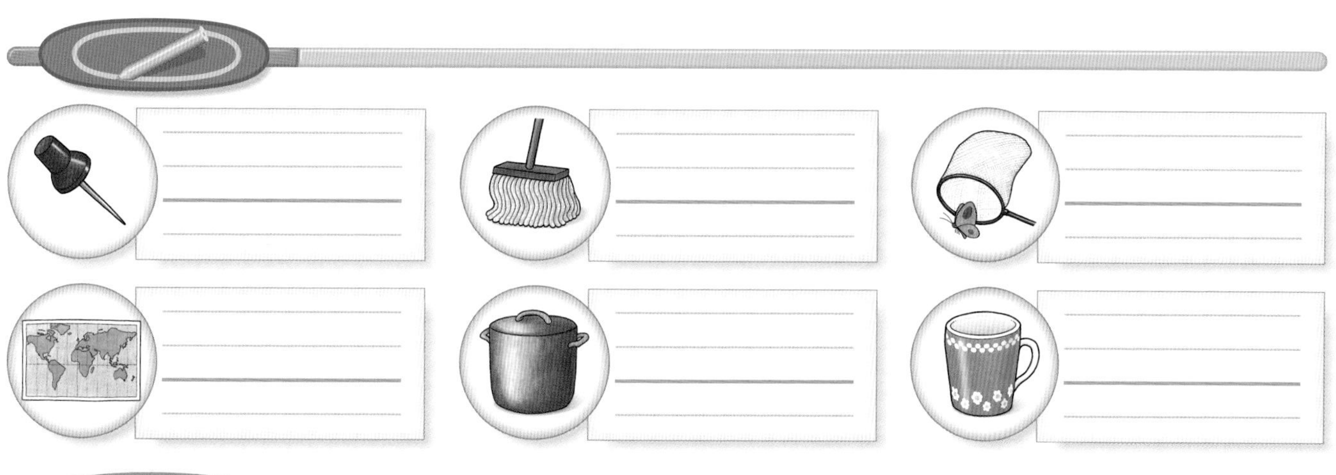

phonics

1 A fat bat can run.

2 A fat bat can sit.

3 A fat bat can hit.

to be continued...

 I'm home.

 Oh, hi.

 Where are you, Dad?

 I'm in the kitchen.
I'm making a salad for dinner.
Come and help me.

 I'm coming.

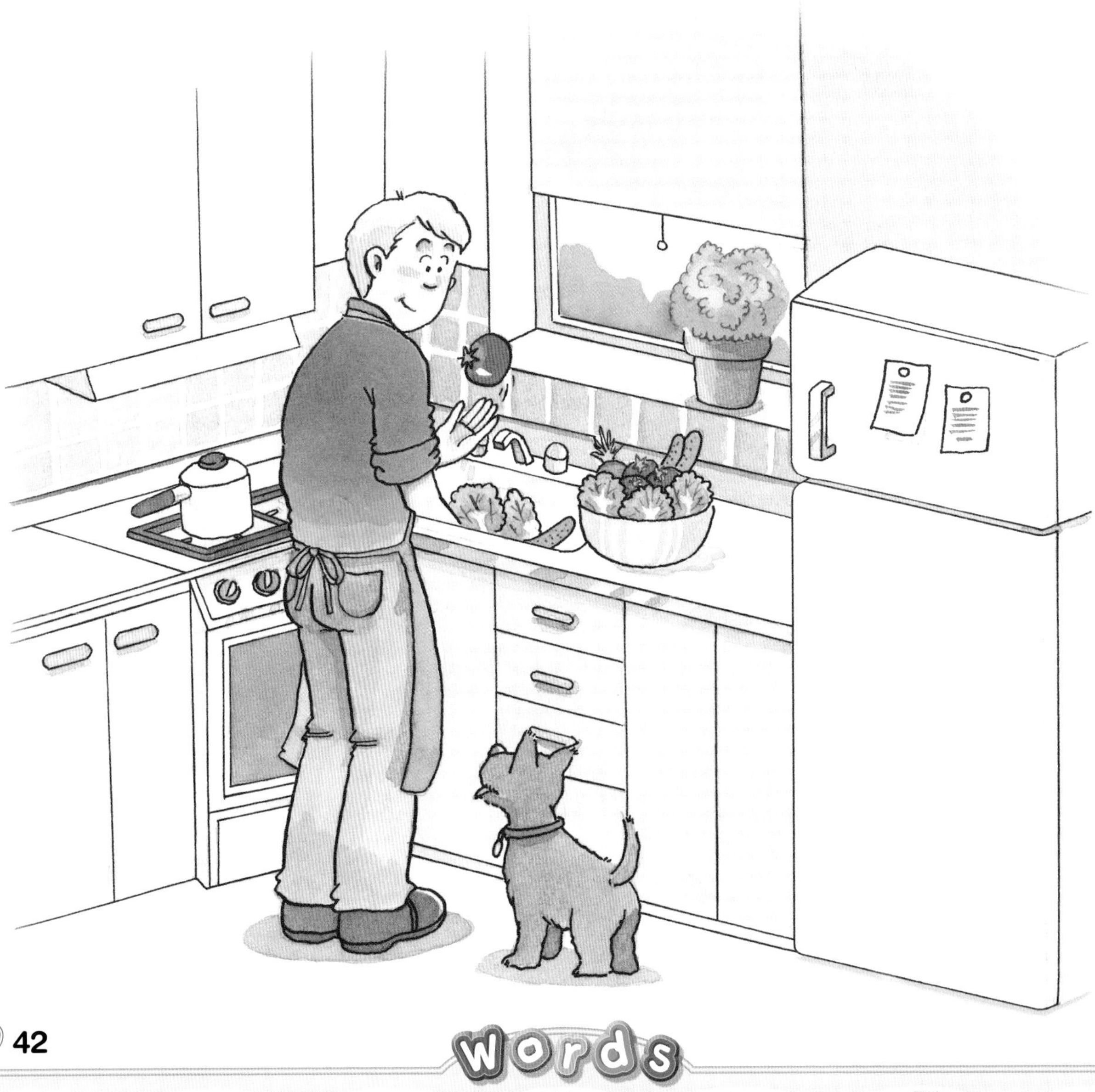

42

Words

kitchen

living room

bedroom

dining room

bathroom

garden

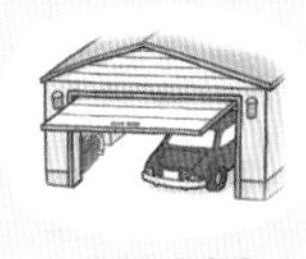
garage

Communication activity

140

- Where is Mark?
- I know. He is in the bedroom.
- What is he doing?
- He is writing a letter.

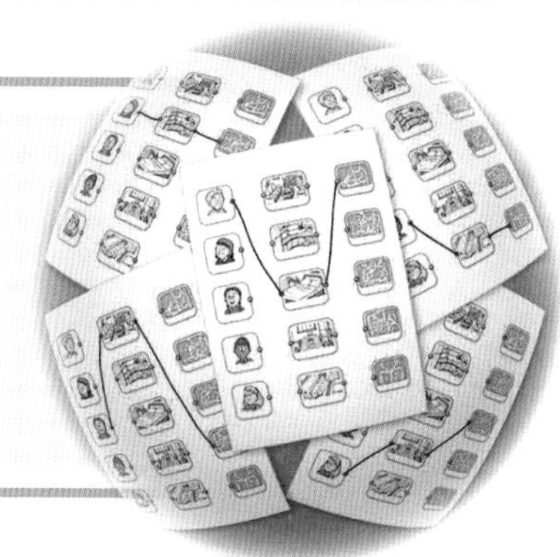

This is my house.

1

2

3

4

5

6

43→44

A salad. A salad.

Let's make a salad.

A salad. A salad.

A delicious salad.

Lettuce, broccoli, cucumbers, too!

Carrots, onions, green peppers, too!

Toss it. Mix it.

Mix it well.

It's delicious!

We can tell!

45

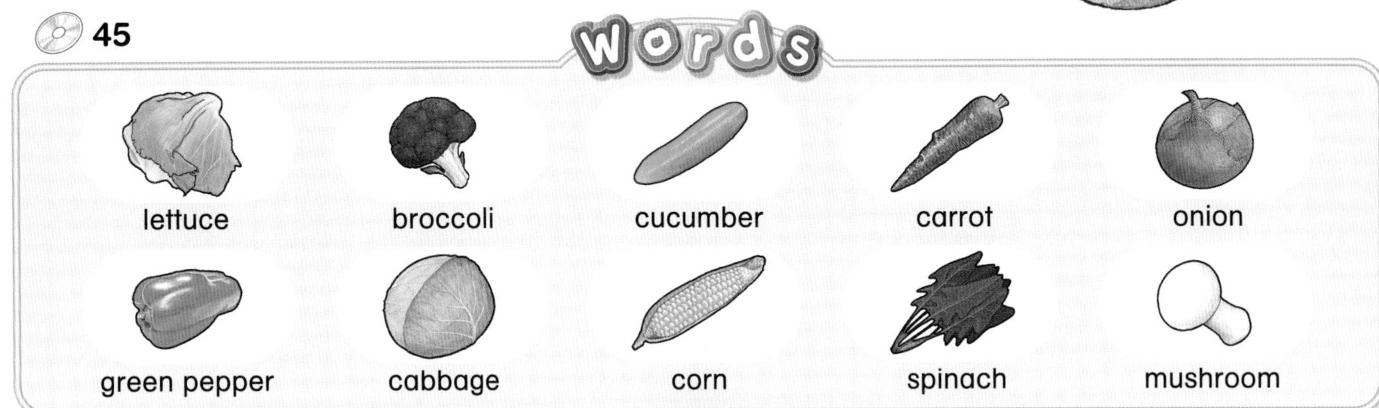

Communication activity

141

- Which is my basket?
- How many tomatoes do you have?
- I have four tomatoes.

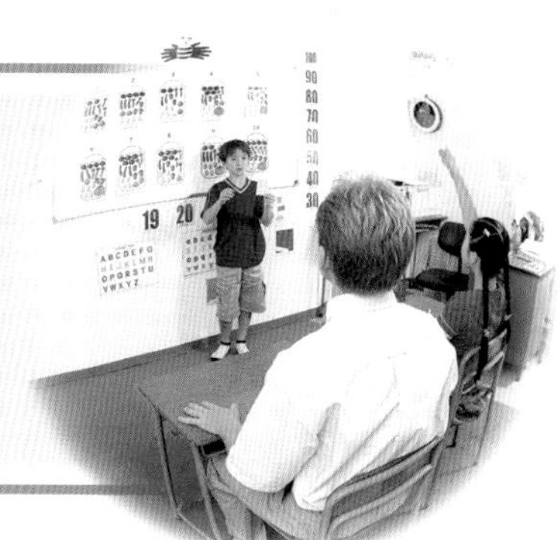

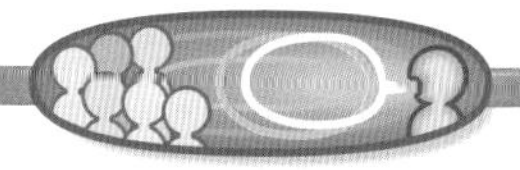

in my salad.

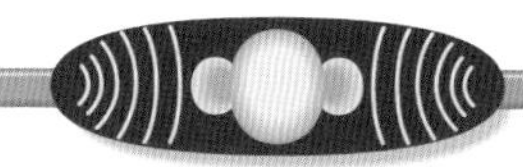

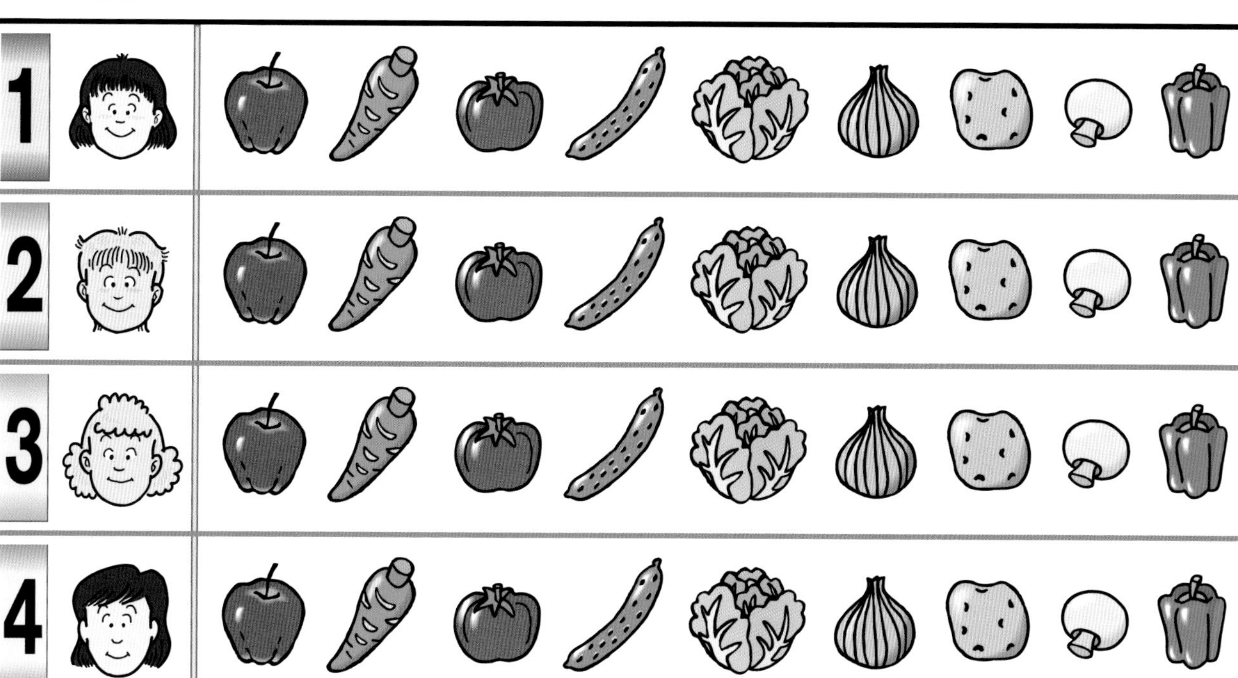

 Pass me the salad, please.

 Here you are.
Do you want more chicken?

 No, thank you. I'm full.

48→49

What do you want to have?

Fried chicken, beef steak, roast pork and a baked fish.

Rice, spaghetti, sandwiches and a hot dog.

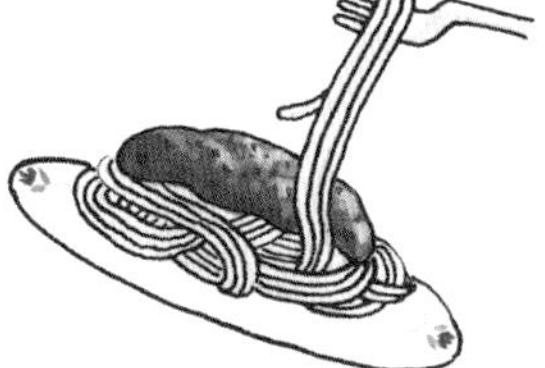
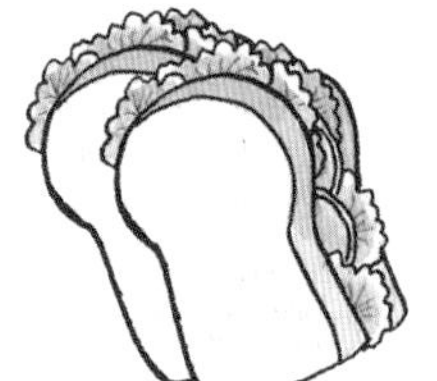

Cheese, yogurt and a big scoop of ice cream.

A cup of coffee and a cup of tea!

Wow!
Isn't that too much?

Communication activity

- What do you want from the grain group?
- I want spaghetti.

142

Food Pyramid

Fats, oil, sugar

Milk Group

Meat & Fish Group

Vegetable Group

Fruit Group

Grain Group

My lunch

phonics

4	5	6

A fat bat can mop.	A fat bat can jump.	But... a fat bat cannot fly.

The END.

Good morning.

It's seven o'clock.

Time to wake up!

Hurry up and change your clothes.

Get your shirt and get your pants.

Hurry up and have your breakfast.

Milk, eggs, bread and butter.

Hurry up and pack your bag.

Pack your pencils and pack your books.

Hurry up and go to school!

See you later. Good bye, Mark!

52

Words

Communication activity

🔊143

- It's seven o'clock. Time to wake up.
  Hurry up and go to school.

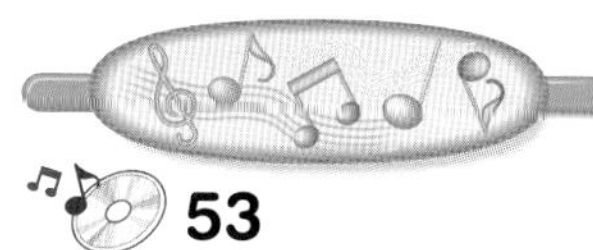

53

This is the way

① This is the way I wash my face, wash my face, wash my face.
This is the way I wash my face, early in the morning.

② This is the way I brush my teeth, brush my teeth, brush my teeth.
This is the way I brush my teeth, early in the morning.

③ comb my hair ④ change my clothes ⑤ eat my toast
⑥ pack my bag ⑦ go to school

① I wake up.

②

③

④

⑤

⑥

⑦

⑧

⑨

⑩

54→55

Where, where, where?

Where shall we go?

To the park, to the park.

Let's go to the park!

When, when, when?

When shall we go?

On Sunday, on Sunday.

Let's go on Sunday!

How, how, how?

How shall we go?

By bike, by bike.

Let's go by bike!

That sounds great!

56

Words

Communication activity

- Where shall we go?
- Let's go to the zoo by balloon at night.

144

by rocket

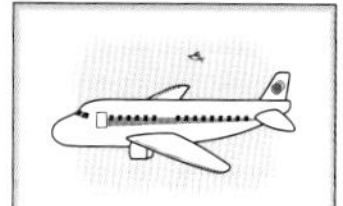
by airplane

by bus

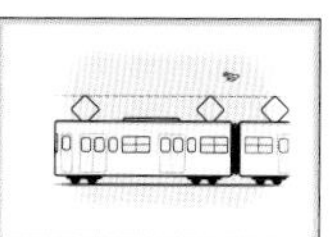
by train

by balloon

by ship

on foot

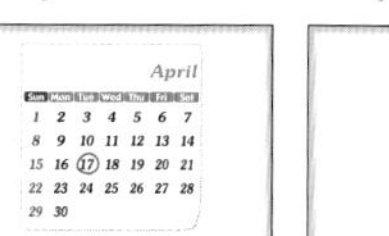

on April 17th

in April

on Wednesday

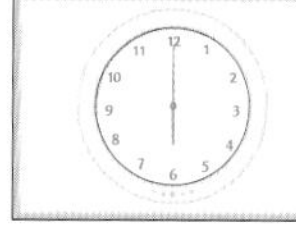
at 6 o'clock

in winter

at night

in the morning

(Where?)

I'll go ______________________

(How?) ______________ (When?) ______________

1

Where?	
When?	
How?	

2

Where?	
When?	
How?	

3

Where?	
When?	
How?	

4

Where?	
When?	
How?	

57→58

It's seven o'clock.

Time to eat supper.

Hurry up and set the table.

Get your fork and get your plate.

Hurry up and finish your supper.

Steak, potatoes, chicken and salad.

Hurry up and do your homework.

Science, English, math and art.

Hurry up and take a bath.

Wash your face and wash your hair.

Hurry up and go to bed.

See you tomorrow. Good night, Mark!

59

Communication activity

145

- What do I do?
- You wash your hair.

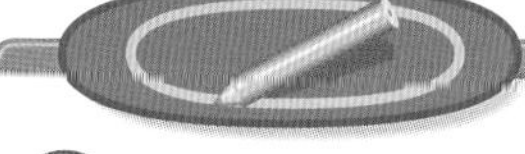

1. Set the table!

2. Finish your supper!

3. Do your homework!

4. Take a bath!

fork math plate English salad spoon
science steak face pizza hair legs

1	2	3

A red bug.	A red bug is wet.	A red bug is mad.

to be continued...

60→61

How is the weather?

Warm and fine, warm and fine,
warm and fine on a spring day.

spring

How is the weather?

Sunny and hot, sunny and hot,
sunny and hot on a summer day.

summer

How is the weather?

Cool and windy, cool and windy,
cool and windy on a fall day.

fall

How is the weather?

Cold and snowy, cold and snowy,
cold and snowy on a winter day.

winter

62

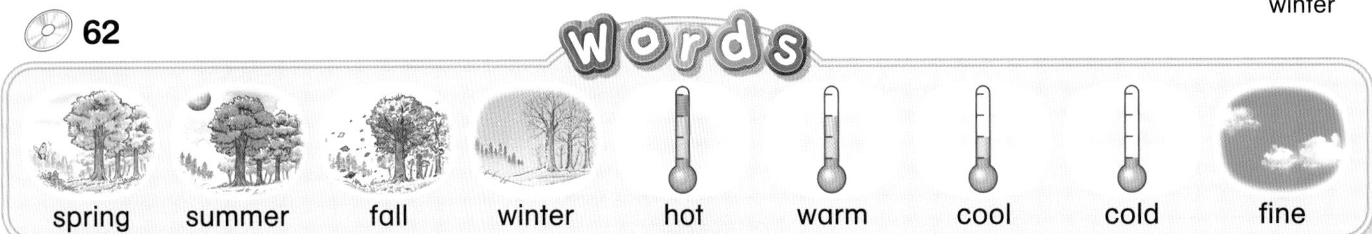

Communication activity

146

- This is the weather report from Canada.
- How is the weather in Canada?
- It's sunny and hot.

country	weather	country	weather
 Canada	and	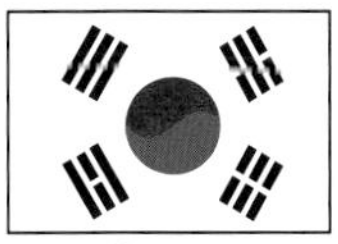 Korea	and
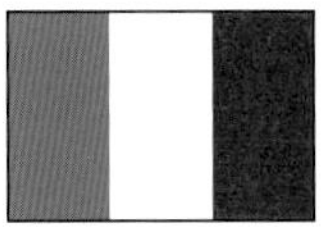 France	and	Thailand	and
 China	and	 India	and
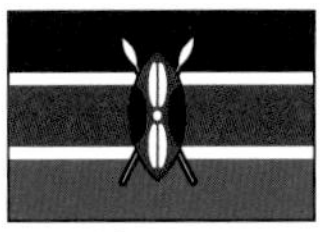 Kenya	and	 Japan	and
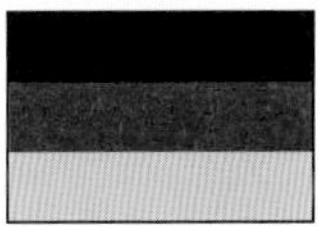 Germany	and	 U.S.A.	and
 Spain	and	 Brazil	and

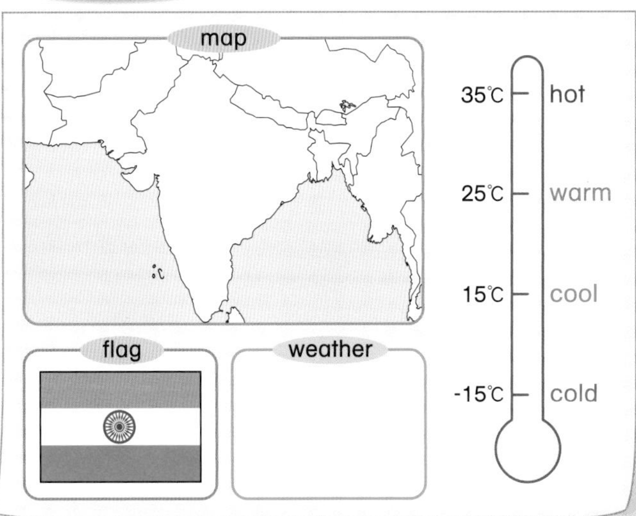

Weather in India

It is ____________

and ____________ .

63→64

What color is the book on the desk?  It's blue. 

What color is the book in the desk?  It's yellow. 

What color is the book under the desk?  It's green. 

What color is the book by the desk?  It's purple. 

Where is the blue book?
It's on the desk.

Where is the yellow book?
It's in the desk.

Where is the green book?
It's under the desk.

Where is the purple book?
It's by the desk.

65

Communication activity

● What color is the book on the desk?

● It's blue.

147

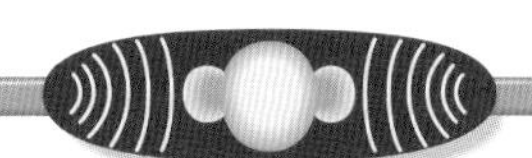

1

a 

b 

c 

2

a 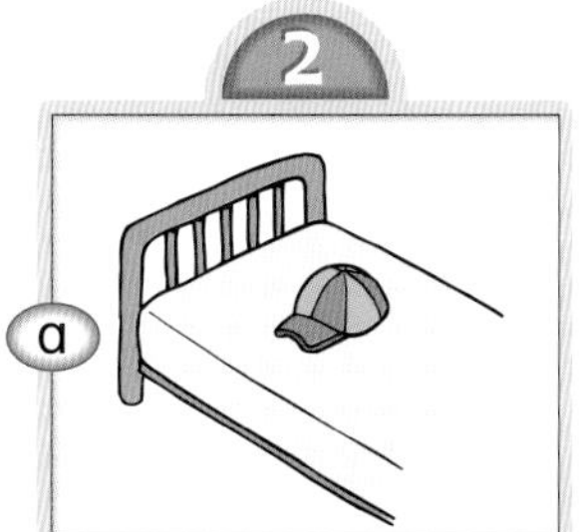

b 

c 

3

a 

b 

c 

4

a 

b 

c 

66→67

What do you have in your bag?

What do you have in your bag?

What do you have in your bag?

Show me what you have.

Textbooks, notebooks, pencils, and an eraser.

No games, no comic books, no snacks, SEE?

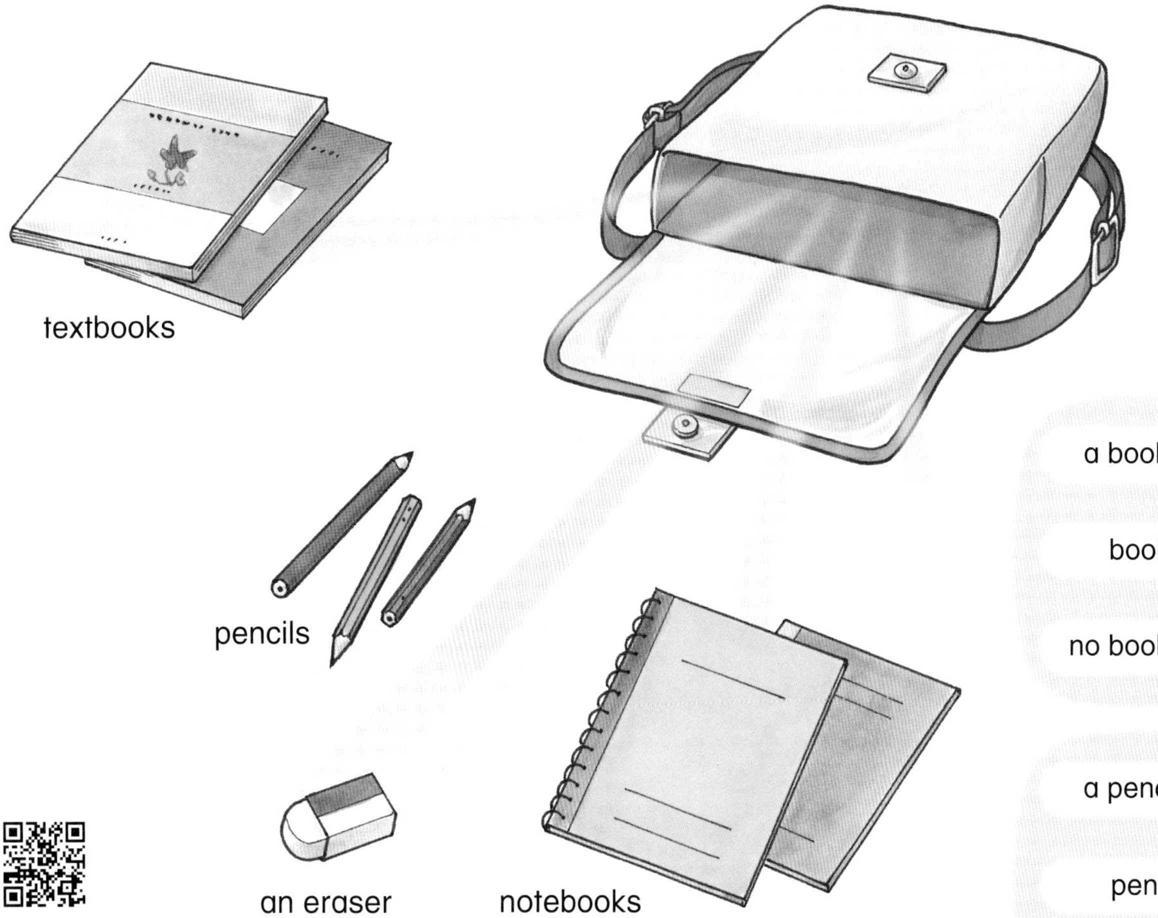

textbooks

pencils

an eraser

notebooks

a book

books

no books

a pencil

pencils

no pencils

68

Words

tissue(s)
handkerchief
key
cell phone
game
comic book
CD
scissors
glue stick
marker(s)
pencil sharpener
sticker(s)
snack(s)
water bottle

Communication activity

- What do you have in your bag?
- Do you have a comic book in your bag?
- Yes, I do. ／ No, I don't.

148

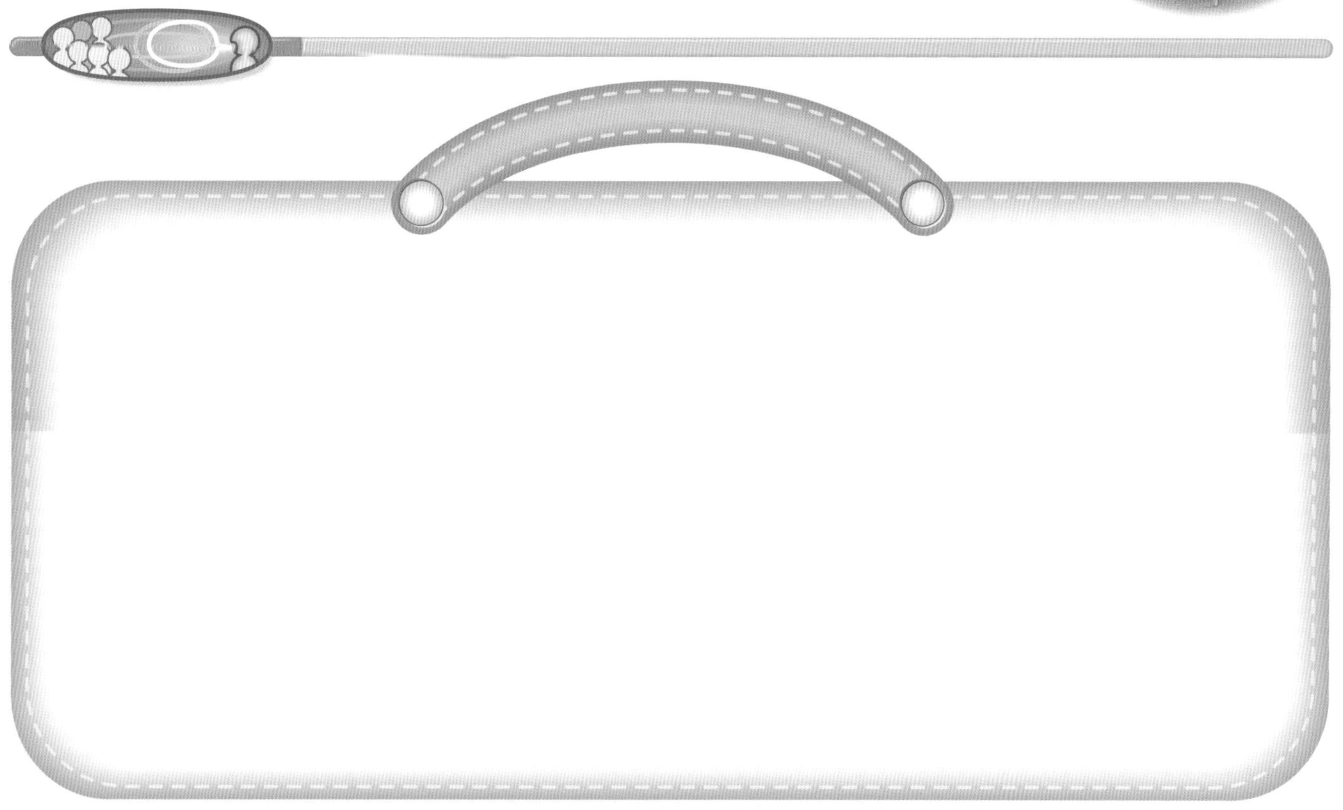

I have ______________________________

______________________________ in my bag.

4	5	6
	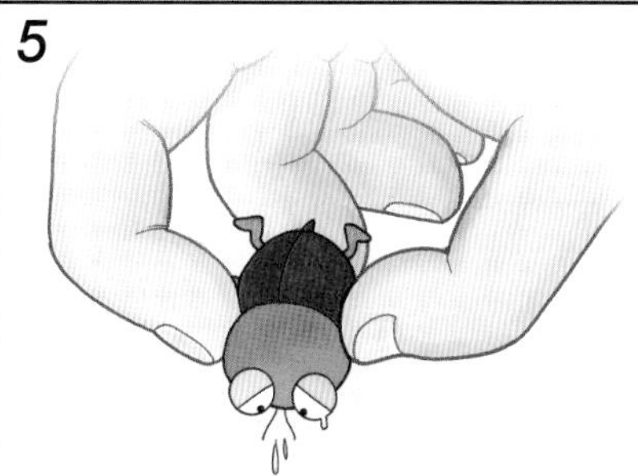	
A red bug is in a net.	A red bug is sad.	A sad red bug is in a box.

to be continued...

69→70

Will you get a ladder for me, please?

Beg your pardon?

Get a ladder for me, please.

Louder, please.

GET A LADDER FOR ME!

Be careful. Watch your step!

Ouch!

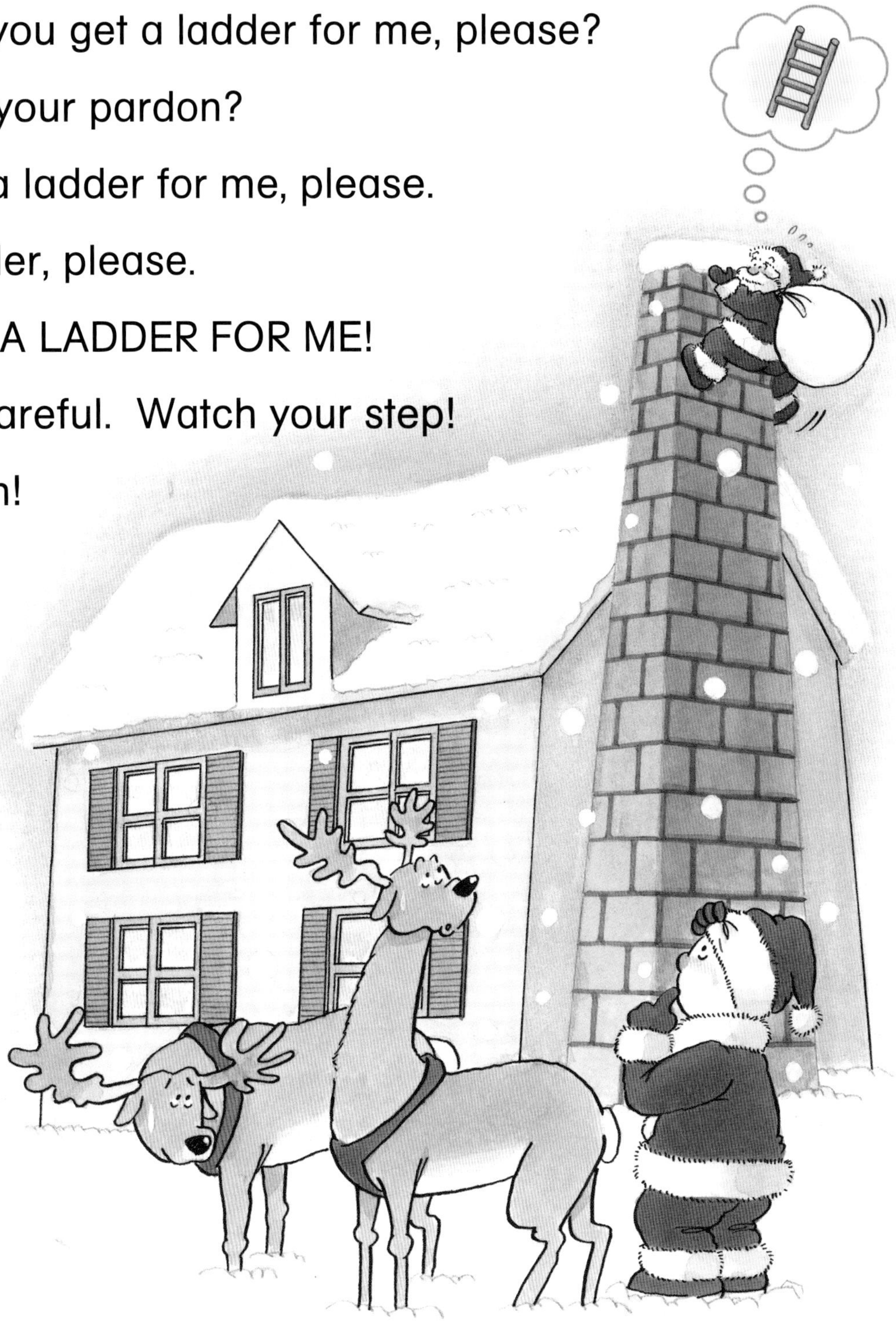

71

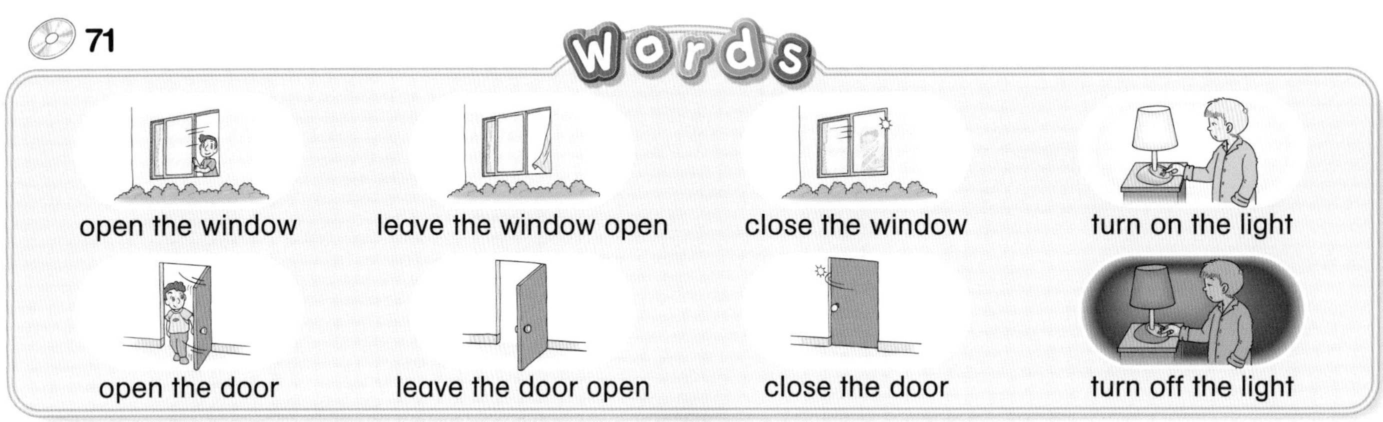

Communication activity

149

- Will you show me your notebook, please?
- Show me your notebook, please.
- Show me your notebook.

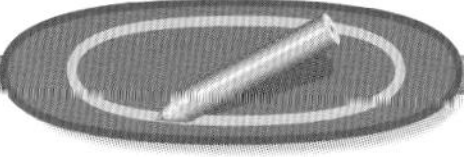

Polite Arrow

Open the window.

Open the window, please.

Will you open the window, please?

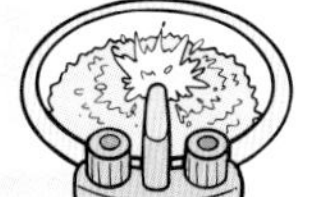

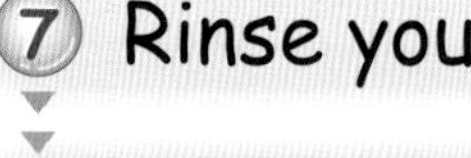

TPR Wash your hands!

102

1. Go to the sink.
2. Turn on the water.
3. Wet your hands.
4. Take the soap.
5. Wash your hands.
6. Put the soap back.
7. Rinse your hands.
8. Turn off the water.
9. Take the towel.
10. Dry your hands.
11. Put the towel back.
12. Show me your hands!

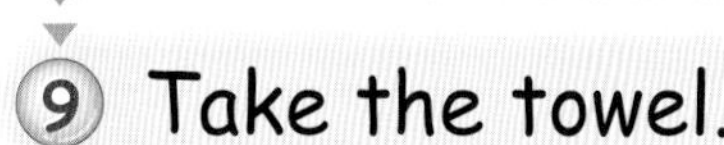
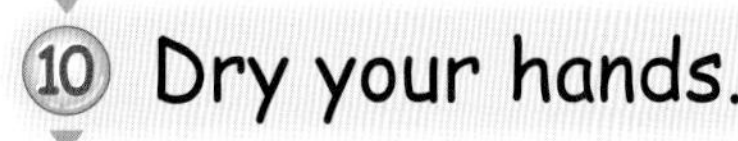
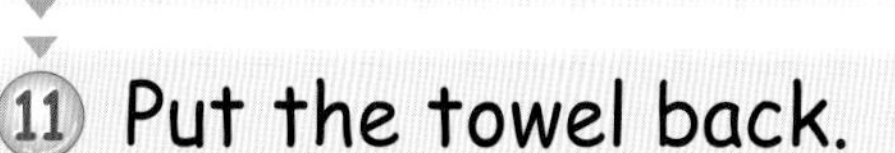

72→73

What a big dog!

What a little dog!

What a long dog!

What a pretty dog!

What a fat dog!

What a dirty dog!

What a scary dog!

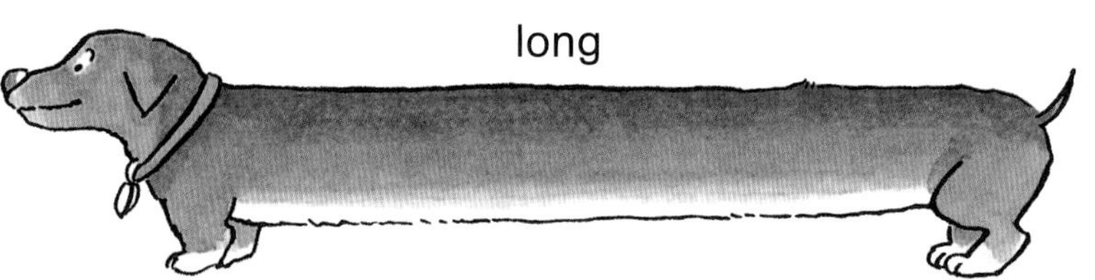

74

Words

strong

weak

tall

short

fat

thin

clean

dirty

young

old

scary

Communication activity

150

- What a long pencil!
- What a short pencil!

What a big ______ !

What a scary ______ !

What a little ______ !

What a pretty ______ !

What a nice teacher!

1

a

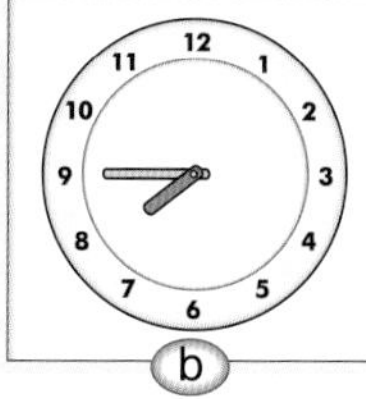

b

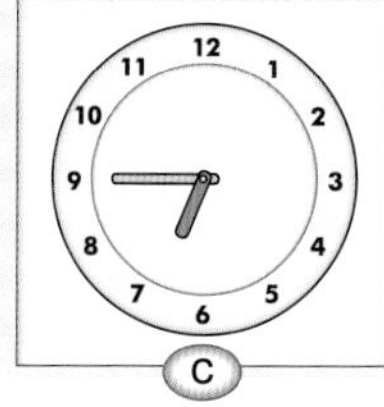

c

2

a

b

c

3

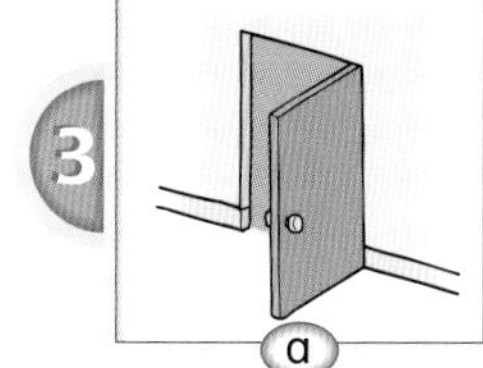

a

b

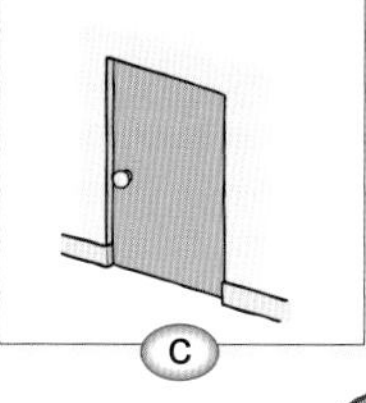

c

4

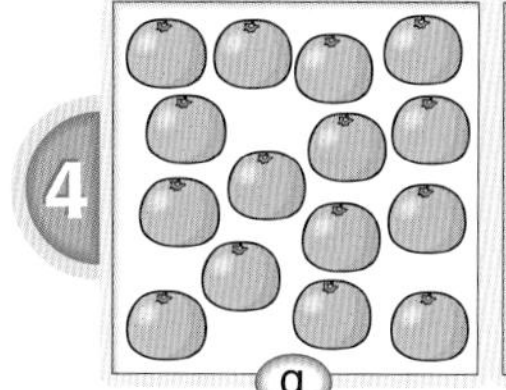

a

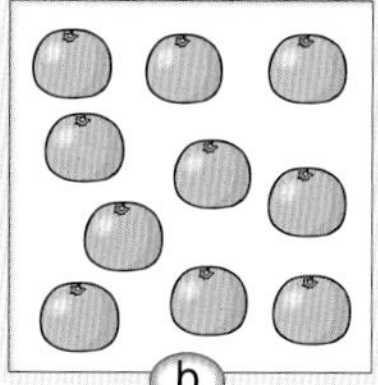

b

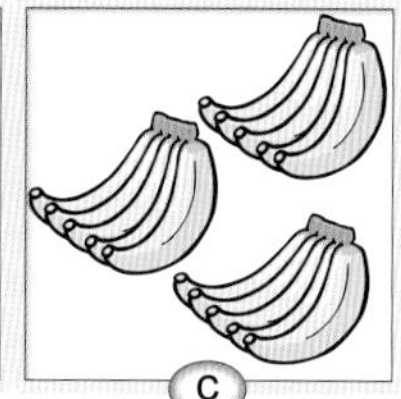

c

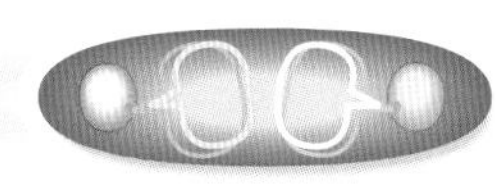

75→76

 May I come in?  Yes, you may.

 May I sit here?  Yes, you may.

 May I join you?  Yes, you may.

 May I play the game?  Yes, you may.

 May we play the game?  No, you may not!

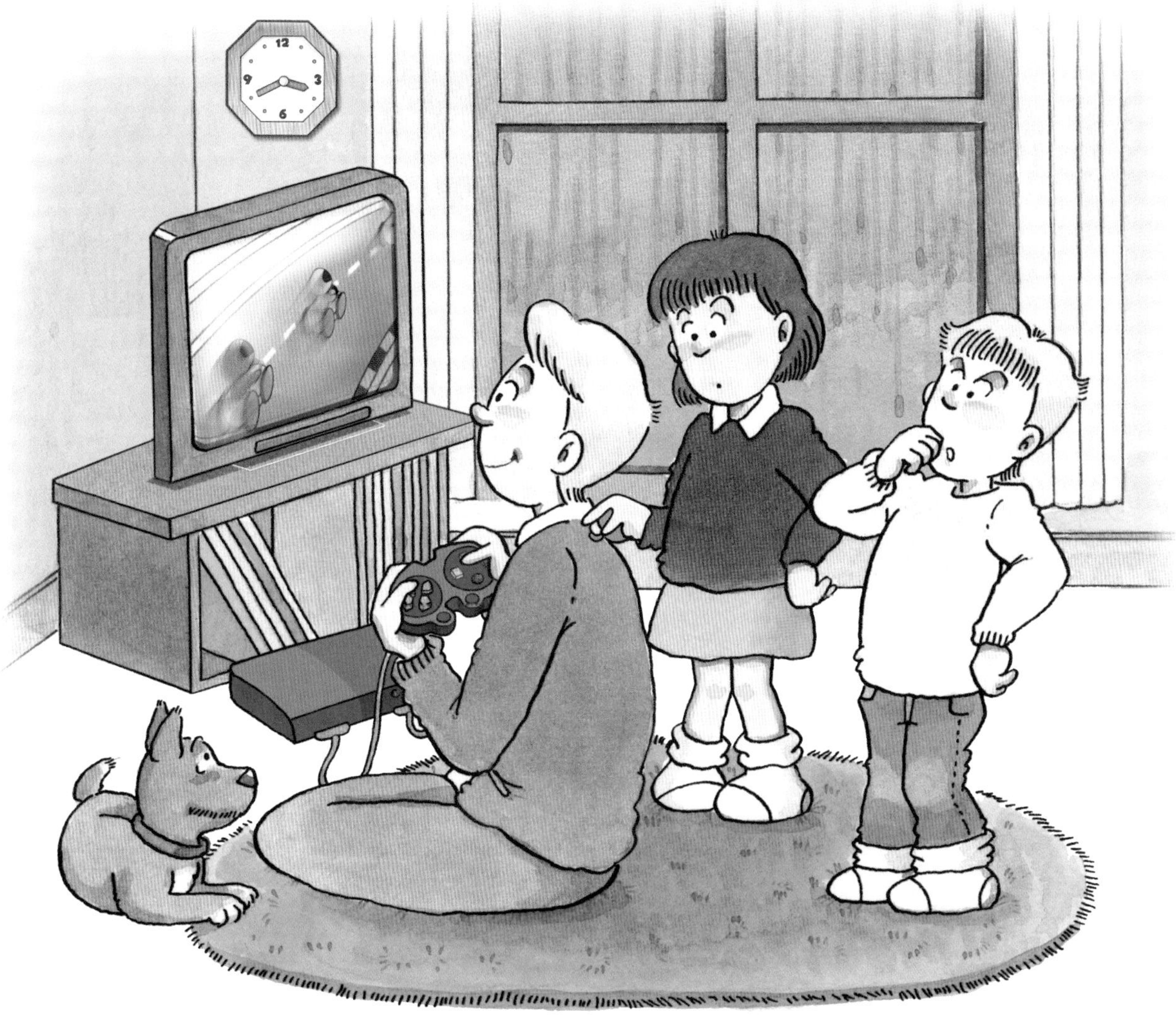

77

Words

Communication activity

151

- May I go up (down)?
- Yes, you may. / No, you may not.

A

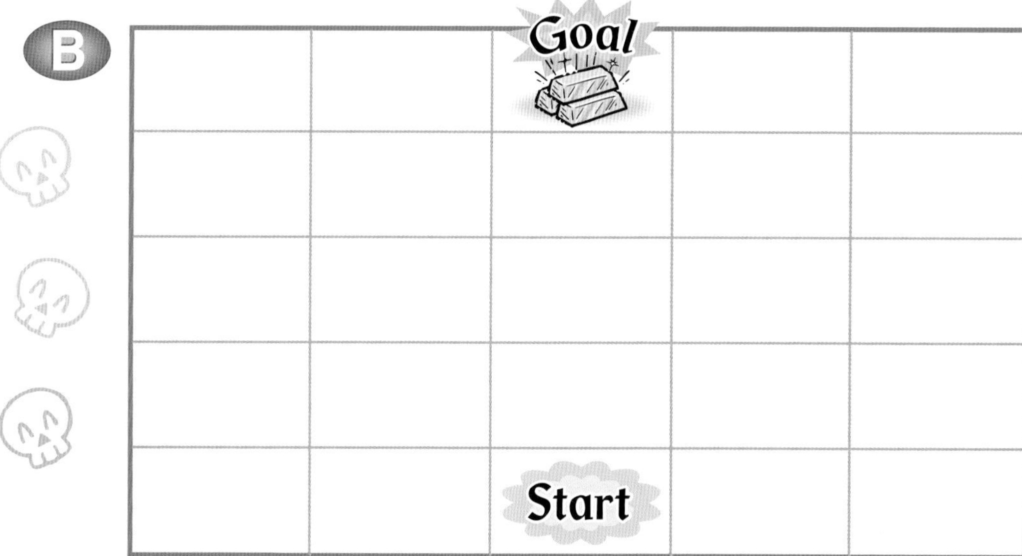

B

7	8	9
A sad red bug is out!	A red bug is not sad.	A red bug is free.

The END.

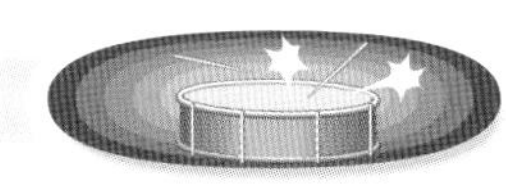

78→79

Yumi likes tennis. Yumi likes tennis. **But...**

Nelson likes judo. Nelson likes judo. **But...**

Min likes skiing. Min likes skiing. **But...**

Ema likes dodgeball. Ema likes dodgeball. **But...**

I like soccer.

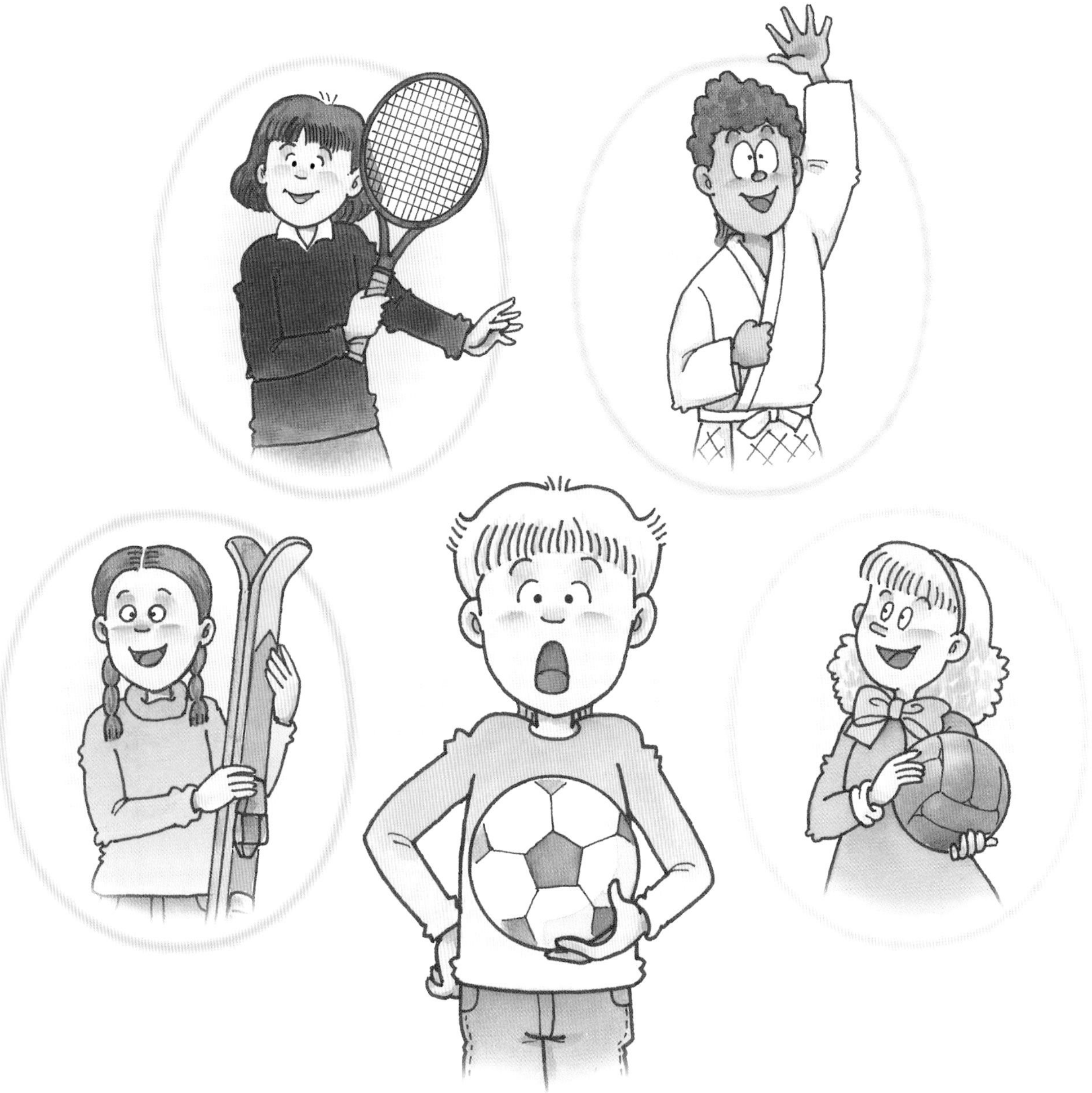

80

Words

tennis | judo | skiing | dodgeball | soccer | basketball | table tennis | baseball | volleyball

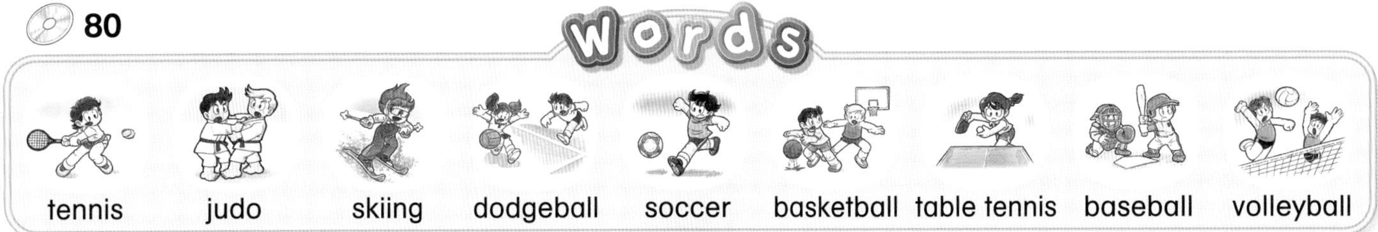

- Terry lives in Vancouver.
- He likes swimming.
- He likes science.

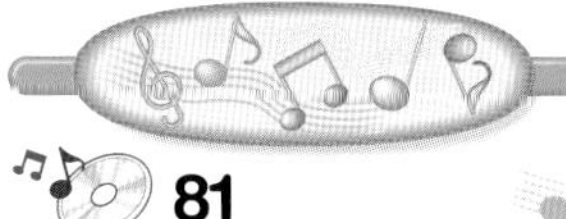

81

Do You Know the Muffin Man?

① *Do you know the muffin man,*
the muffin man, the muffin man?
Oh, do you know the muffin man,
who lives on Drewery Lane?

② *Oh, yes I know the muffin man,...*

What is your name?	
Where do you live?	
What sport do you like?	
What school subject do you like?	

This is my friend.

(His, Her) name is ________________

(He, She) lives in ________________

(He, She) likes ________________

82→83

Who has a birthday in January?

I have my birthday in January.

Yumi has her birthday in January.

Who has a birthday in March?

I have my birthday in March.

Mark has his birthday in March.

84

Words

1st first	2nd second	3rd third	4th fourth	5th fifth	6th sixth	7th seventh	8th eighth	9th ninth	10th tenth
11th eleventh	12th twelfth	13th thirteenth	14th fourteenth	15th fifteenth	16th sixteenth	17th seventeenth	18th eighteenth	19th nineteenth	20th twentieth
21st twenty-first	22nd twenty-second	23rd twenty-third	24th twenty-fourth	25th twenty-fifth	26th twenty-sixth	27th twenty-seventh	28th twenty-eighth	29th twenty-ninth	30th thirtieth
31st thirty-first									

Communication activity

153

- When is your birthday?
- My birthday is January 10th.
- You are the first in line.

name	birthday	name	birthday

________ is the first in line. ________ is the second in line…
name name

85

1 January

2 February

3 March

4 April

5 May

6 June

7 July

8 August

9 September

10 October

11 November

12 December

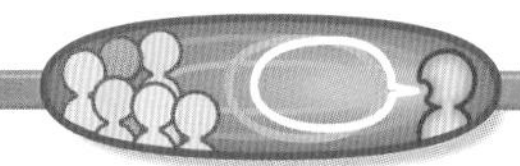

A Surprising Present

You: Happy birthday! This is for you.

friend: Thank you. May I open it?

You: Go ahead.

friend: Wow! What a nice ________!

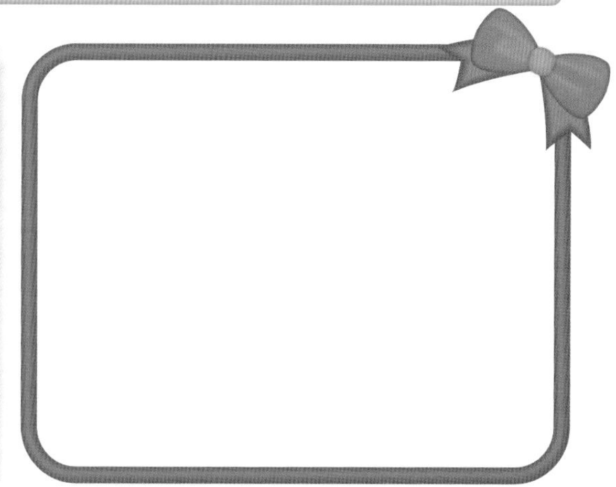

Phonics

103

ch

church
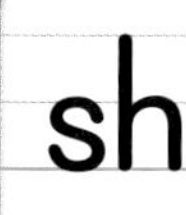
rich

sh

sheep

ship

th

math

father

mother

86→87

We are twenty-five years old.

Mark is a cook.

Yumi is a teacher.

Nelson is a dentist.

Min is a florist.

Ema is a scientist.

88

Words

cook

teacher

dentist

florist

scientist

nurse

soccer player

baker

cartoonist

cabin attendant

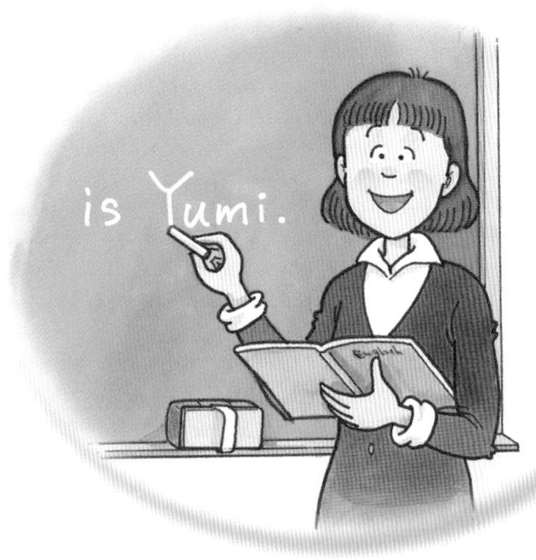

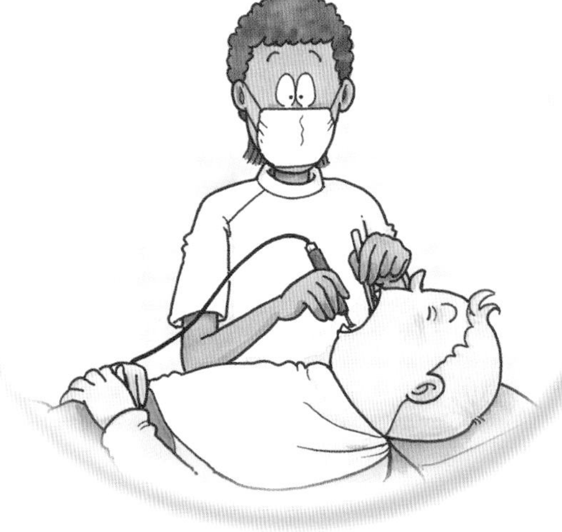

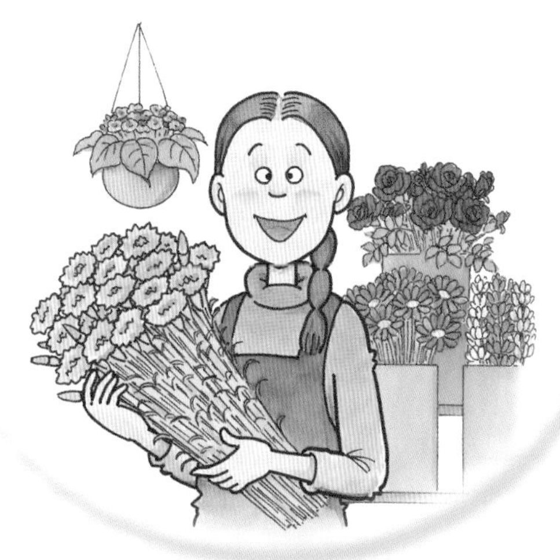

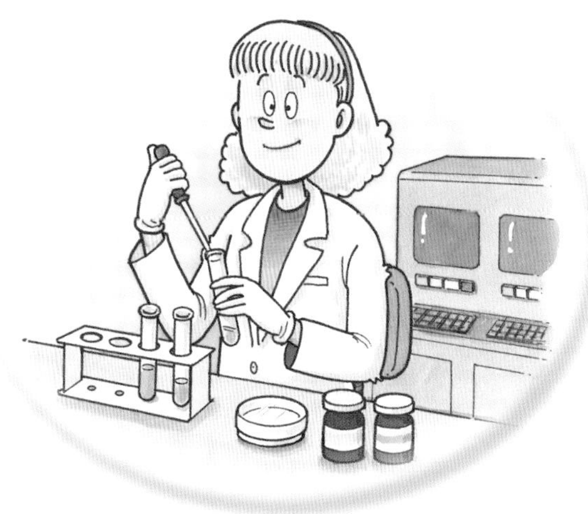

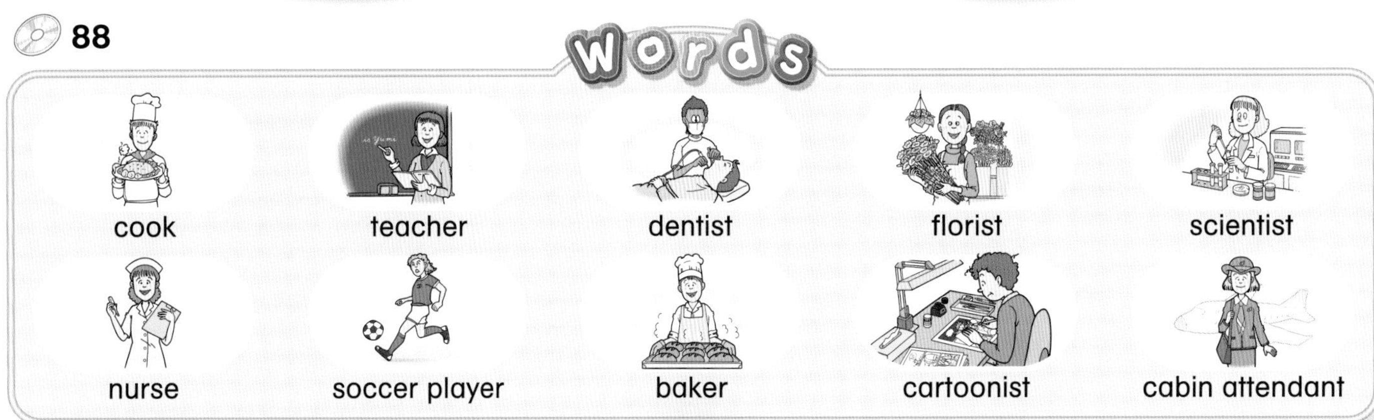

Communication activity

154

- What do you do?
- I am a teacher.
- She is a teacher.

Hello. My name is ____________.

I am twenty-five years old.

I am a ____________.

Thank you.

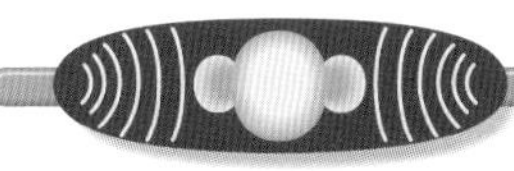

1

a

b

c

2

a

b

c

3

a

b

c

4

a

b

c

1 An elephant is walking.
He is hungry.

2 He finds an apple tree.
"It looks nice!"

3 He wants an apple,
but he can't climb the tree.
But he can't climb the big tall tree.

4 A monkey is in the tree.
He takes one!

5 The monkey says to the elephant,
"Here. Have one."

6 The elephant says to the monkey,
"Let's share it!"
"Yes, one half for you and one half
for me."

Communication activity

●155

- Can you swim?
- Yes, I can.
  No, I can't.

1	Can you …?	①	②	③
2	Do you have …?	①	②	③
3	Do you like …?	①	②	③
4	Do you want …?	①	②	③

1. I can ______________________________
2. I have ______________________________
3. I like ______________________________
4. I want ______________________________

In a Cabin in the Woods

1 In a cabin in the woods,

2 A little man was standing by the window.

3 A little rabbit was hopping by, knocking at the door.

4 "Help me, help me, help! Before the hunter shoots me dead."

5 The little man let him in, saying, "Little rabbit, little rabbit, come inside."

6 "In my house, it is safe and here you can hide."

156

- What color is his shirt?
- It is yellow.
- What color are his pants?
- They are gray.

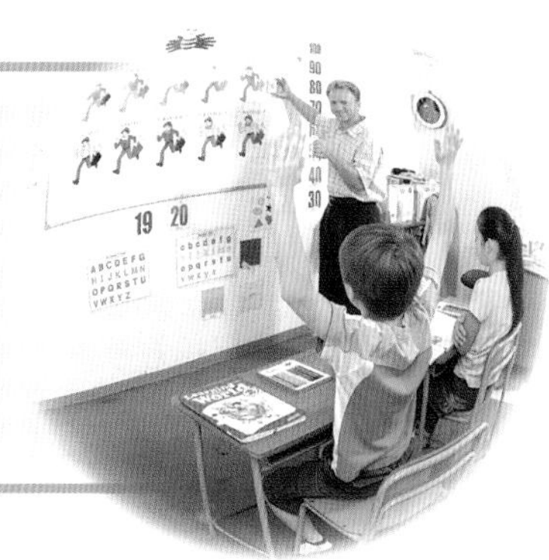

1 His hat is ____________.

2 His scarf is ____________.

3 His shirt is ____________.

4 His belt is ____________.

5 His bag is ____________.

6 His pants are ____________.

7 His shoes are ____________.

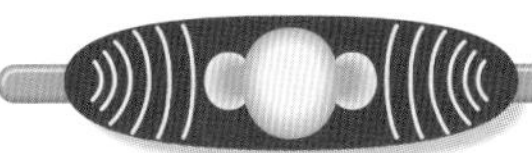

1

a

b

c

2

a

b

c

3

a

b

c

4
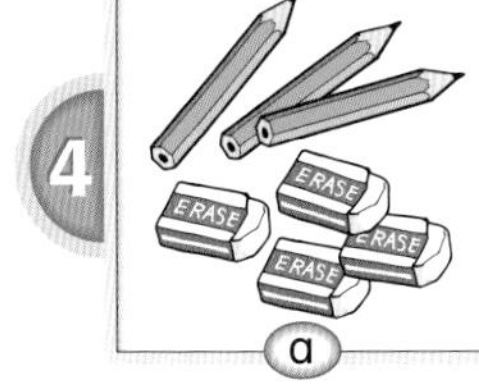
a

b
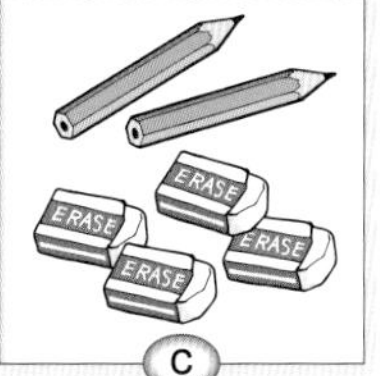
c

94→95

Hello.

My name is Yumi.

My family name is Suzuki.

I am nine years old.

My birthday is January fifteenth.

I live in Vancouver.

I am from Kobe, Japan.

I like dogs.

I don't like spiders.

I want to be a teacher.

This is my friend, Mark.

His family name is Cates.

He is eight years old.

His birthday is March sixth.

He lives in Vancouver.

He likes parrots.

He wants to be a cook.

Communication activity

157

- This is my friend.
- She is ten years old.
- She lives in Osaka.
- She likes turtles.

name	me	my friend
How old are you?		
When is your birthday?		
Where do you live?		
What animal do you like?		
What do you want to be?		

a 

b  

c 

a 

b 

c 

a 

b 

c 

Let's talk about the pictures.

A

p.

B

p.

C

p.

D

p.

E

p.

絵を見ていくつ英文で言えるかな?

In picture ______, ______________

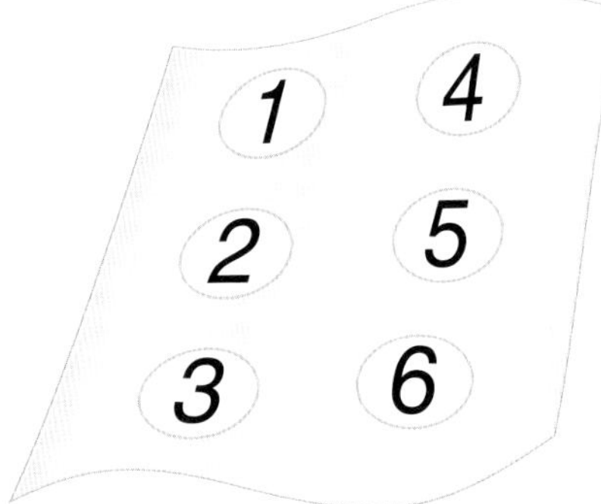

英文を言うごとに番号に色をぬりましょう。

Let's read.

A

B

C
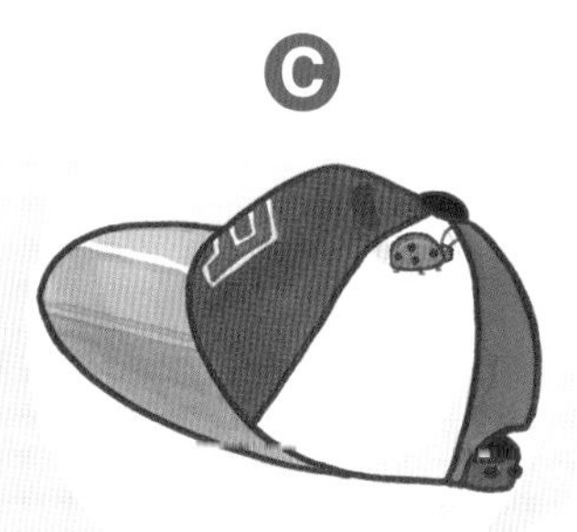

D

1. a bad bat on a bat (　　)
2. six pigs jumping on the bed (　　)
3. It is a big cat. (　　)
4. A red bug is on a cap. (　　)
5. A hen and a cat sit on a bus. (　　)
6. A pink pig sat on a pin. Ouch! (　　)
7. Wash your hands with soap. (　　)
8. Six rich men sit on a bus. (　　)
9. She can hug the sun. (　　)
10. My mother can speak French. (　　)

E

F

G

J

I

H

words words words ...and more!

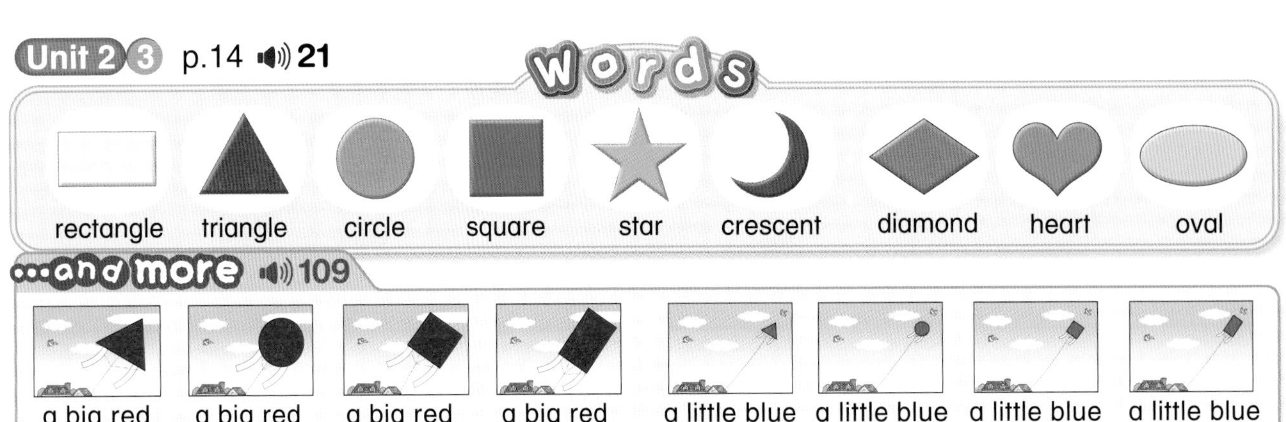

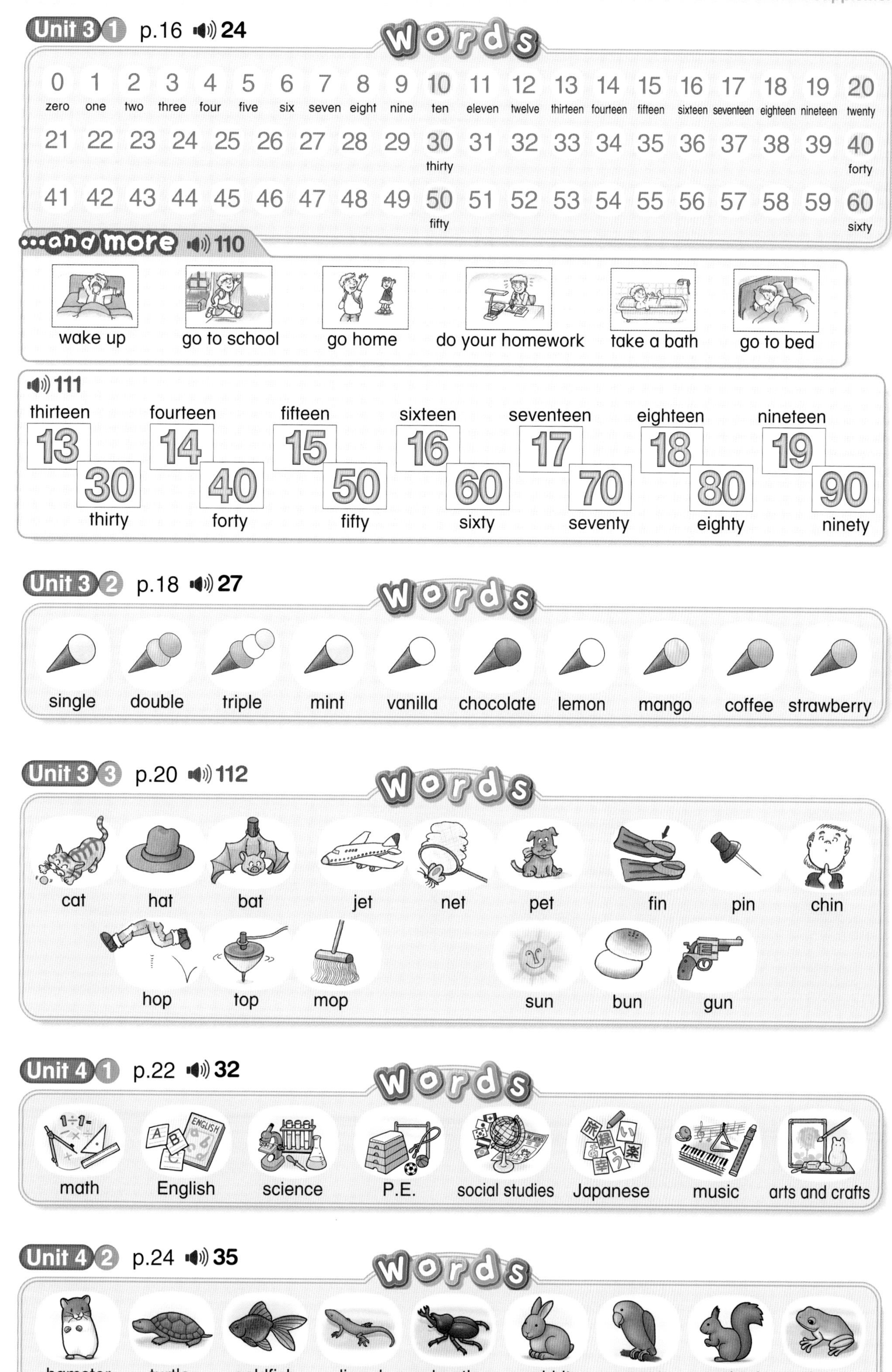

Unit 3 1 p.16 24
Words
0 1 2 3 4 5 6 7 8 9 10 11 12 13 14 15 16 17 18 19 20
zero one two three four five six seven eight nine ten eleven twelve thirteen fourteen fifteen sixteen seventeen eighteen nineteen twenty
21 22 23 24 25 26 27 28 29 30 31 32 33 34 35 36 37 38 39 40
thirty forty
41 42 43 44 45 46 47 48 49 50 51 52 53 54 55 56 57 58 59 60
fifty sixty
...and more 110
wake up
go to school
go home
do your homework
take a bath
go to bed
111
thirteen 13 30 thirty
fourteen 14 40 forty
fifteen 15 50 fifty
sixteen 16 60 sixty
seventeen 17 70 seventy
eighteen 18 80 eighty
nineteen 19 90 ninety
Unit 3 2 p.18 27
Words
single
double
triple
mint
vanilla
chocolate
lemon
mango
coffee
strawberry
Unit 3 3 p.20 112
Words
cat
hat
bat
jet
net
pet
fin
pin
chin
hop
top
mop
sun
bun
gun
Unit 4 1 p.22 32
Words
math
English
science
P.E.
social studies
Japanese
music
arts and crafts
Unit 4 2 p.24 35
Words
hamster
turtle
goldfish
lizard
beetle
rabbit
parrot
squirrel
frog

Unit 4 ③ p.26 113 Words

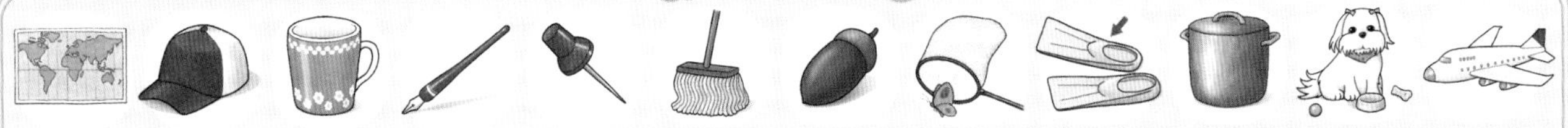

map cap cup pen pin mop nut net fin pot pet jet

Unit 5 ① p.28 42 Words

kitchen living room bedroom dining room bathroom garden garage

...and more 114

writing a letter washing cleaning (vacuuming) eating watching TV reading a book

Unit 5 ② p.30 115 Words

lettuce broccoli cucumber carrot onion tomato potato

green pepper cabbage corn spinach mushroom apple

Unit 5 ③ p.32 116 Words

fried chicken beef steak roast pork baked fish rice spaghetti a sandwich

a hot dog cheese yogurt a big scoop of ice cream a cup of coffee a cup of tea

...and more 117 Food Pyramid

oil sugar milk ice cream cheese yogurt butter

fish egg chicken beef carrot onion lettuce

cucumber eggplant pumpkin apple orange banana grapes

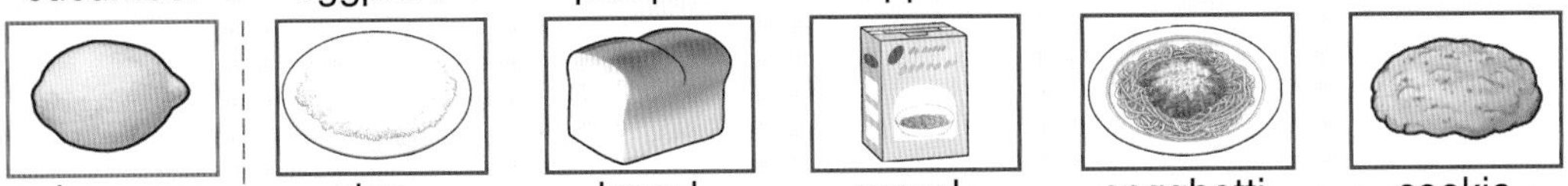

lemon rice bread cereal spaghetti cookie

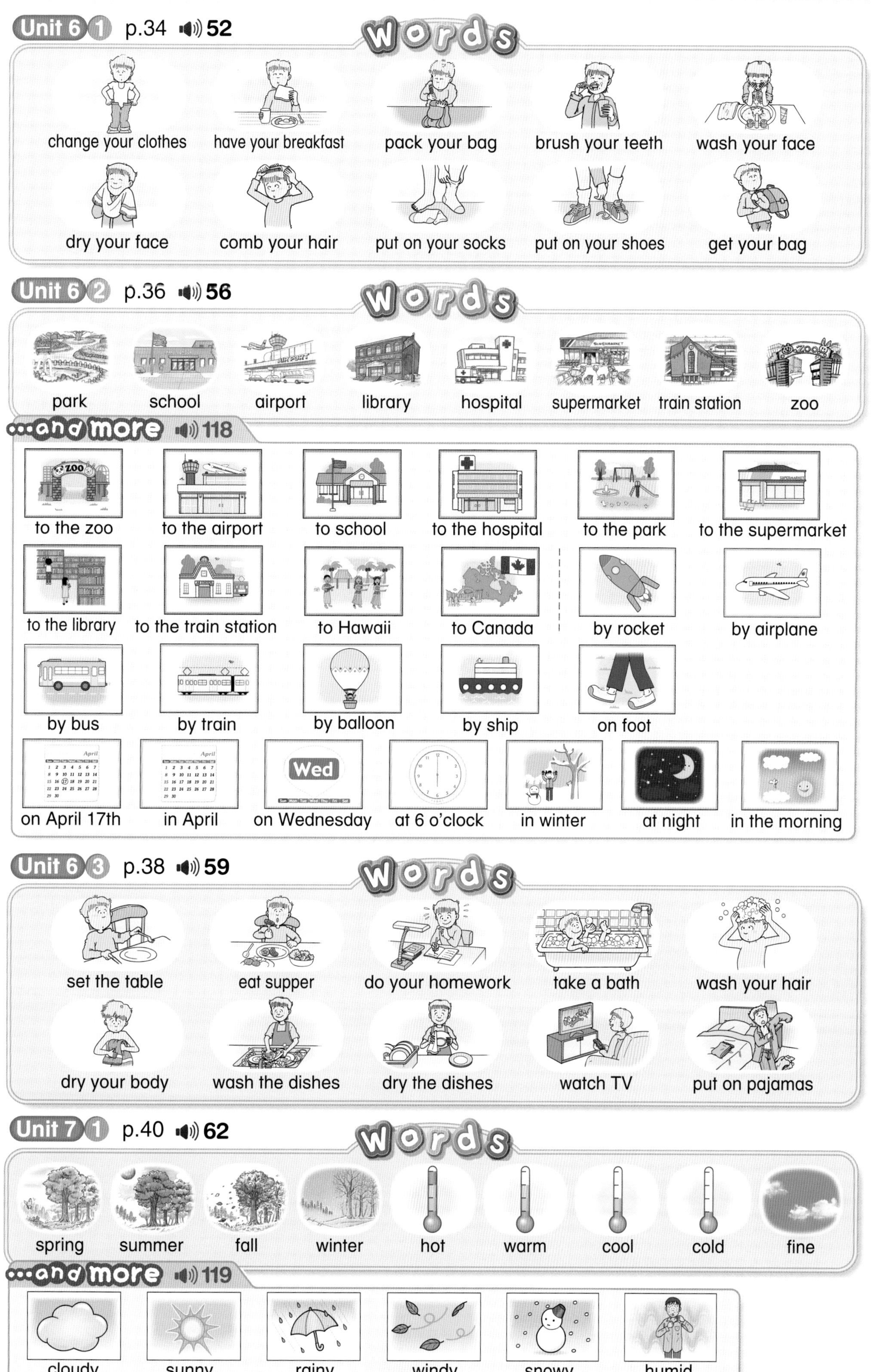
Unit 6 1 p.34 52
Words
change your clothes
have your breakfast
pack your bag
brush your teeth
wash your face
dry your face
comb your hair
put on your socks
put on your shoes
get your bag
Unit 6 2 p.36 56
Words
park
school
airport
library
hospital
supermarket
train station
zoo
...and more 118
to the zoo
to the airport
to school
to the hospital
to the park
to the supermarket
to the library
to the train station
to Hawaii
to Canada
by rocket
by airplane
by bus
by train
by balloon
by ship
on foot
on April 17th
in April
Wed
on Wednesday
at 6 o'clock
in winter
at night
in the morning
Unit 6 3 p.38 59
Words
set the table
eat supper
do your homework
take a bath
wash your hair
dry your body
wash the dishes
dry the dishes
watch TV
put on pajamas
Unit 7 1 p.40 62
Words
spring
summer
fall
winter
hot
warm
cool
cold
fine
...and more 119
cloudy
sunny
rainy
windy
snowy
humid

Unit 7 2 p.42 120

on	in	under	by	over	between

on the desk	in the desk	under the desk	by the desk	over the desk	between the desks

Unit 7 3 p.44 68

Words

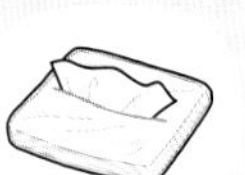

tissue(s)

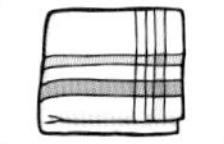
handkerchief

key

cell phone

game

comic book

CD

scissors

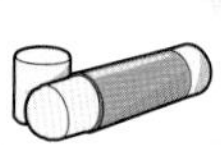
glue stick

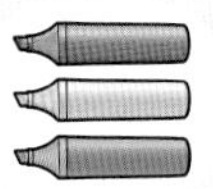
marker(s)

pencil sharpener

sticker(s)

snack(s)

water bottle

...and more 121

a book

books

no books

a pencil

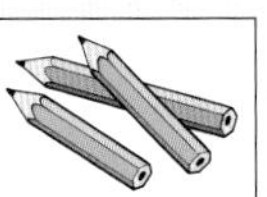
pencils

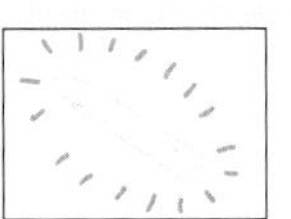
no pencils

Unit 8 1 p.46 71

Words

open the window

leave the window open

close the window

turn on the light

open the door

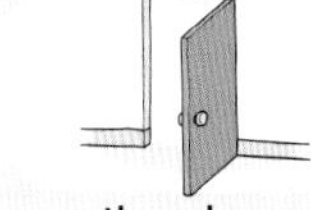
leave the door open

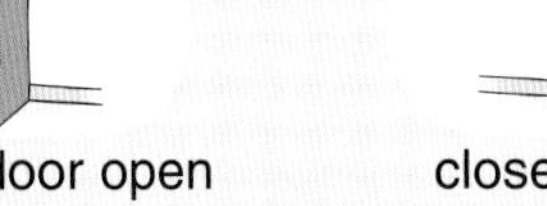

close the door

turn off the light

Unit 8 2 p.48 74

Words

strong weak

tall

short

fat

thin

clean dirty

young

old

scary

...and more 122

big

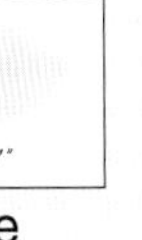
little

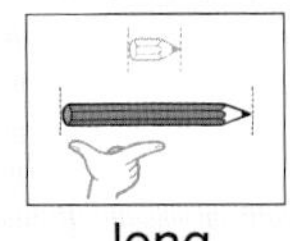
long

short

Unit 8 3 p.50 77

Words

play the game

play the CD

use the computer

use a dictionary

come in

go out

speak Japanese

...and more 123

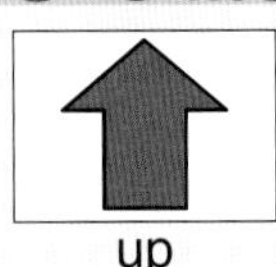
up

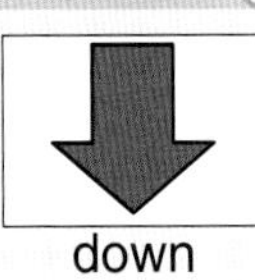
down

left

right

Unit 9 1 p.52 80

Words

tennis judo skiing dodgeball soccer basketball table tennis baseball volleyball

Unit 9 2 p.54 124

Words

January February March April May June

July August September October November December

84

1st	2nd	3rd	4th	5th	6th	7th	8th	9th	10th
first	second	third	fourth	fifth	sixth	seventh	eighth	ninth	tenth
11th	12th	13th	14th	15th	16th	17th	18th	19th	20th
eleventh	twelfth	thirteenth	fourteenth	fifteenth	sixteenth	seventeenth	eighteenth	nineteenth	twentieth
21st	22nd	23rd	24th	25th	26th	27th	28th	29th	30th
twenty-first	twenty-second	twenty-third	twenty-fourth	twenty-fifth	twenty-sixth	twenty-seventh	twenty-eighth	twenty-ninth	thirtieth
31st									
thirty-first									

...and more 125

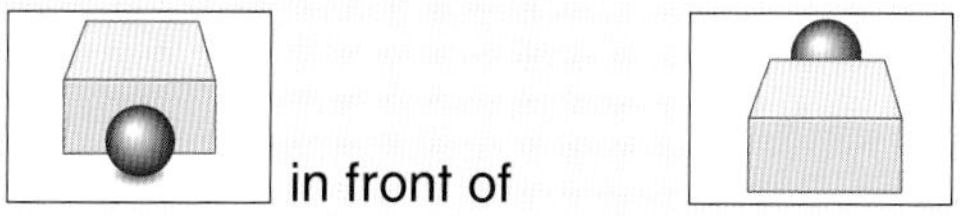

in front of behind

Unit 9 3 p.56 88

Words

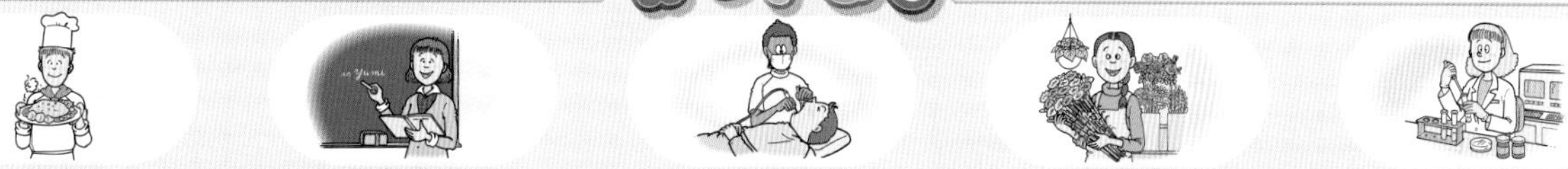

cook teacher dentist florist scientist

nurse soccer player baker cartoonist cabin attendant

Unit 10 1 p.58 ...and more 126

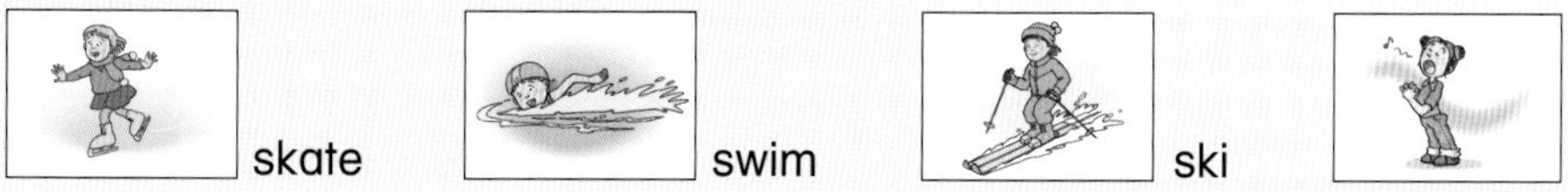

skate swim ski sing

Unit 10 2 p.60 ...and more 127

hat shirt pants shoes belt scarf bag

Let's read.

A Fat Bat

158

1	2	3

A fat bat can run.	A fat bat can sit.	A fat bat can hit.

4	5	6

A fat bat can mop.	A fat bat can jump.	But... a fat bat cannot fly.

The END.

A Red Bug

159

1	2	3

A red bug.	A red bug is wet.	A red bug is mad.

4	5	6
	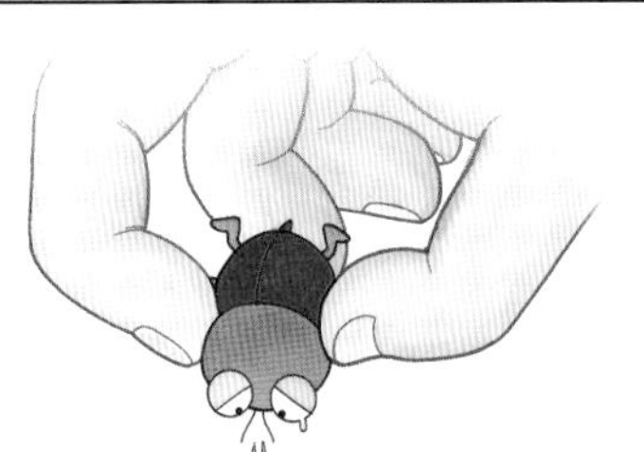	
A red bug is in a net.	A red bug is sad.	A sad red bug is in a box.

7	8	9

A sad red bug is out!	A red bug is not sad.	A red bug is free.

The END.

Song Vegetable Man

by Catherine Steele

99

Vegetable Man. Vegetable Man.
A vegetable man that's what I am.
Vegetable Man. Vegetable Man.
Vegetable Man that's me.

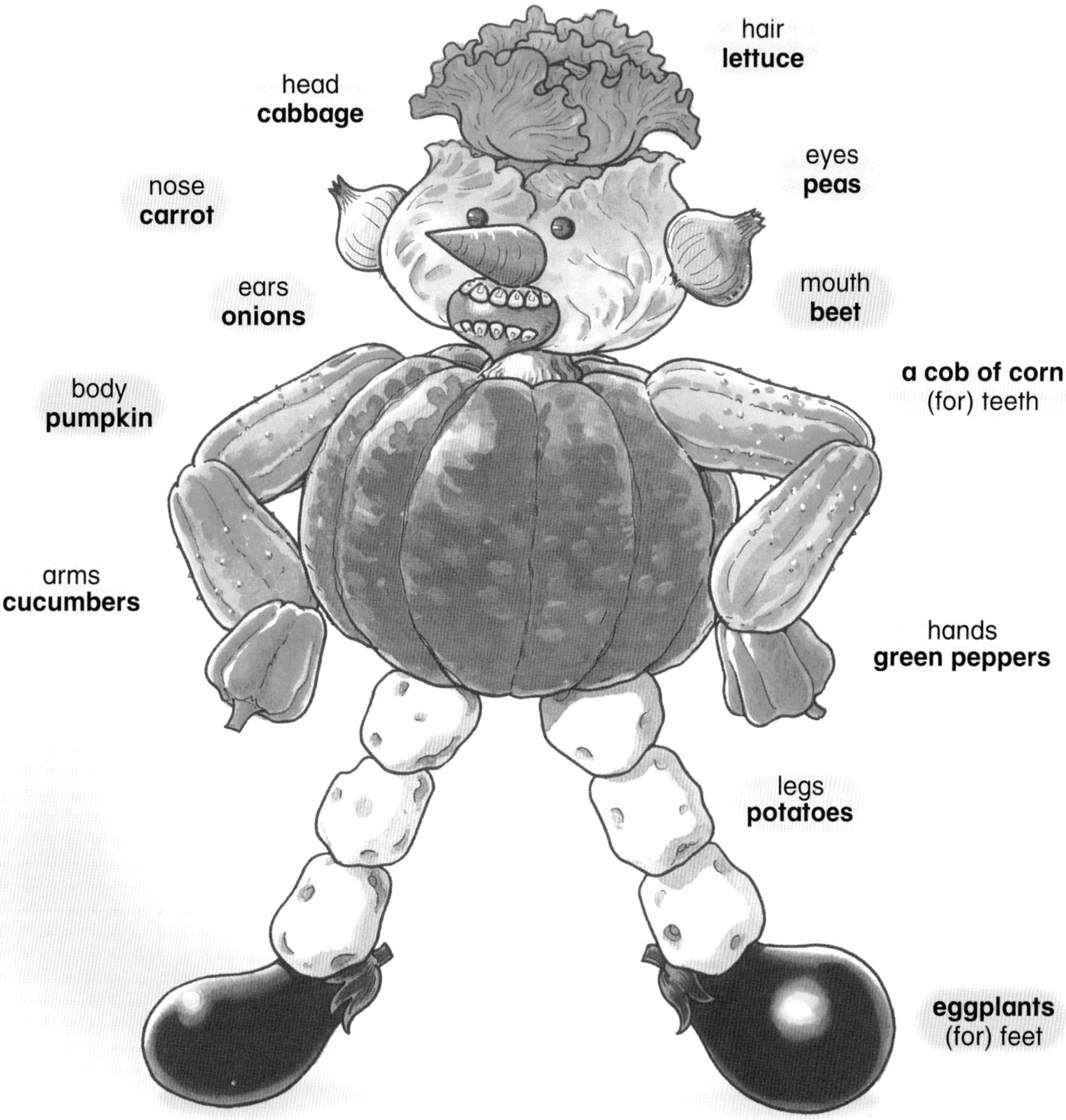

hair **lettuce**

head **cabbage**

eyes **peas**

nose **carrot**

ears **onions**

mouth **beet**

a cob of corn (for) teeth

body **pumpkin**

arms **cucumbers**

hands **green peppers**

legs **potatoes**

eggplants (for) feet

-  My head is a 
-  My ears are 
-  My body is a 
-  My eyes are
- My arms are 
-  My legs are
-  My nose is a 
- 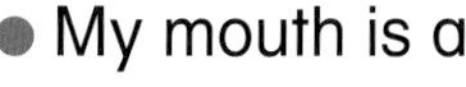 My mouth is a 
-  My hair is a 
-  I have a cob of for teeth.
-  My hands are 
- I have  for feet.

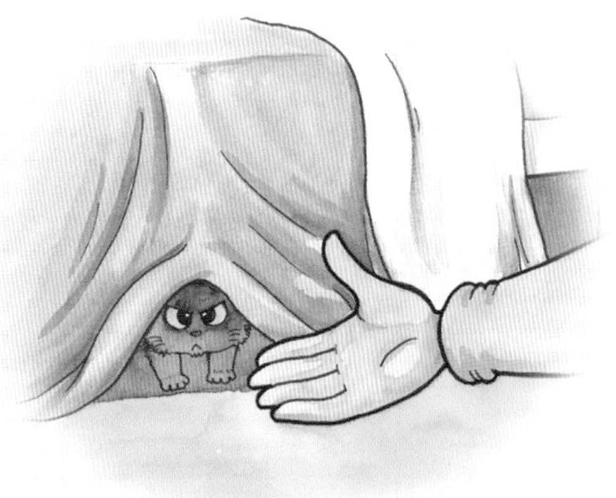

My Kitty is up in the tree.
My Kitty is under the bed.
My Kitty is between the fences.
Oh, she cannot come back to me!

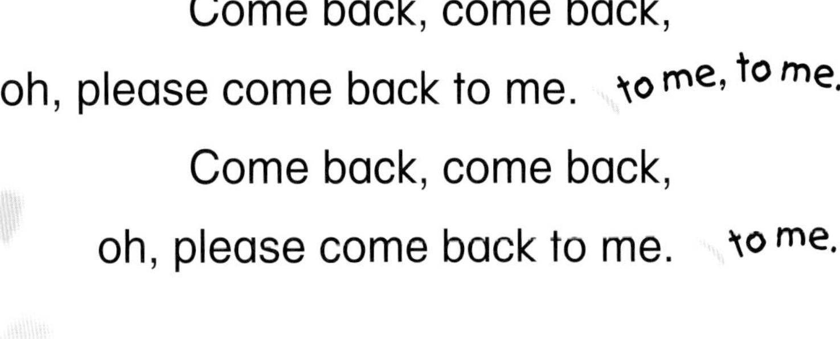

Come back, come back,
oh, please come back to me. to me, to me.
Come back, come back,
oh, please come back to me. to me.

Jack-o'-Lantern

🔊97

I am a pumpkin, big and round.
Once upon a time, I grew on the ground.
Now I have a mouth,
two eyes, and a nose.
What are they for,
do you suppose?
With a candle inside,
shining bright,
I'll be a jack-o'-lantern
on Halloween night.

We Wish You a Merry Christmas

🔊98

We wish you a merry Christmas, ※
we wish you a merry Christmas,
we wish you a merry Christmas,
and a Happy New Year!

Good tidings to you,
wherever you are,
good tidings for Christmas,
and a Happy New Year.

※repeat

Verbs in Use

Say with the Rhythm

104

No.	Unit	Page	Verb	Example
1	Unit 3-1	p.17	go	I usually go to bed at nine. ふつうは9時に寝ます。
2	Unit 3-1	p.16	take	It's time to take a bath. おふろに入る時間です。
3	Unit 3-2	p.18	have	Can I have an ice cream cone, please? アイスクリームコーンをください。
4	Unit 4-3	p.27	know	I know! わかった!
5	Unit 5-1	p.28	come	I'm coming. すぐそっちに行くよ。
6	Unit 5-1	p.28	help	Come and help me. 来ててつだって。
7	Unit 5-2	p.30	make	Let's make a salad. サラダを作りましょう。
8	Unit 5-2	p.30	tell	I can tell! 任せて。わかるよ! やっぱりね!
9	Unit 5-3	p.32	pass	Pass me the salt, please. お塩を取ってください。
10	Unit 6-1	p.34	hurry	Hurry up and do your homework. 急いで宿題をしなさい。
11	Unit 6-1	p.34	change	Hurry up and change your clothes. 急いで着がえなさい。
12	Unit 6-1	p.34	pack	Hurry up and pack your bag. 急いでかばんにつめなさい。
13	Unit 6-2	p.36	sound	That sounds great! それはすばらしいね!
14	Unit 6-3	p.38	finish	I'm finished! 終わりました!
15	Unit 7-3	p.44	see	See? ね、そうでしょう?
16	Unit 8-1	p.47	show	Will you show me your notebook? 私にノートを見せてくれませんか。
17	Unit 8-1	p.46	get	Get a ladder for me, please. はしごを取ってください。
18	Unit 8-1	p.46	watch	Watch your step! 足元に気をつけて!
19	Unit 8-3	p.50	join	May I join you? 私も一緒にしてもいいですか。
20	Unit 8-3	p.50	sit	Can I sit here? ここすわっていい?
21	Unit 10-1	p.58	have	Have one, please. おひとつどうぞ。
22	Unit 10-1	p.58	look	It looks good! おいしそう! いい感じ!
23	Unit 10-1	p.58	share	Let's share it. わけましょう。
24	Unit 10-1	p.58	walk	I walk to school. 私は歩いて学校に行きます。
25	Unit 10-2	p.60	knock	Please knock on the door before entering. 入る前にドアをノックしてください。

Classroom A to Z

Say with the Rhythm

A	After you.	お先にどうぞ。
B	Bring your notebook.	ノートを持ってきなさい。
C	Come here.	ここに来て。
D	Draw a line.	線を引きなさい。
E	Erase the board.	ボード(の文字)を消しなさい。
F	Find your seat.	自分の席を見つけなさい。
G	Get in line.	(列に)ならびなさい。
H	Hand it over.	それを(順に)手渡して。
I	I know.	わかった。
J	Just a moment.	ちょっと待って。
K	Keep your hands off.	さわらないで。
L	Listen to me.	(私の言うことを)よく聞いて。
M	Me, too.	私もです。
N	Nice to meet you.	はじめまして。
O	Open your textbook to page 9.	テキストの9ページを開きなさい。
P	Put your book away.	本をしまいなさい。
Q	Quick! Quick! Hurry up!	はやく! はやく! いそいで!
R	Repeat after me.	後について言いなさい。
S	See you!	またね! また会いましょう。
T	Take a card.	カードを1枚取りなさい。
U	Understand?	わかった?
V	Very good.	よくできました。
W	Write your name.	名前を書きなさい。
X	Excellent!	すばらしい!
Y	You're welcome.	どういたしまして。
Z	Zip your lips.	口を閉じなさい。しずかにしなさい。

A After you.

C Come here.

E Erase the board.

H Hand it over.

K Keep your hands off.

P Put your book away.

X Excellent!

W Write your name.

T Take a card.

Learning World ② Syllabus

Unit	Topics	Grammar	Structures	Words and Phrases レッスンで使うおもな語彙（太字はwordsコーナーの語彙）	Phonics
1-1	友だちとぼく My friend and me	●復習	■My name is .... ■My family name is .... ■I live in .... ■How do you spell ...?	**a-z**	Alphabet train
1-2	いろいろな国の友だち Friends from all over the world	●世界のあいさつ	■I'm from .... ■Nice to meet you.	**Canada, Japan, Korea, Brazil, France** / Bangladesh, Palau / China, Kenya, Germany, Spain, Thailand, India / Hello. Bonjour. Ni hao. Hujambo. Guten Tag. Buenos dias. Annyeong hasimnikka. Sawas dee. Namaste. Konnichiwa.	
1-3	友だちの名前 Friends' names	●代名詞の所有格	■What's his(her) name? ■His(Her) name is		first letter of the words
2-1	地球人としてのぼくたち We are on the same planet.	●現在進行形 ●身近な動詞のing形	■I'm ...ing. ■You are ...ing. ■He is ...ing. ■She is ...ing.	**walking, singing, dancing, writing, reading, speaking, studying, drawing, working, teaching** flying, hopping, walking, eating, jumping, running, sitting, sleeping, swimming	
2-2	調子はどう？ How are you?	●体調を表す形容詞 ●頻度を表す副詞　always	■How is ...? ■He is always .... ■Is Mark sleepy? ■Yes, he is. / No, he isn't.	**sleepy, fine, hungry, tired, angry, happy, sad, sick, full, thirsty**	
2-3	形、しぜん Which kite is Min's?	●形を表す語彙、所有格 ●Whichで始まる疑問文	■Which is your kite? ■Is it a triangle? ■Yes, it is. / No, it isn't. ■That is Min's kite.	**rectangle, triangle, circle, square, star, crescent, diamond, heart, oval** / kite	
3-1	ぼくの1日 My day	●身近な動詞句 ●数字　1～60 ●頻度を表す副詞　usually	■Time to wake up. ■I usually ... ■How do you go from 1 to 30? ■I go from ...	**zero, one, two, three, four, five, six, seven, eight, nine, ten, eleven, twelve, thirteen, fourteen, fifteen, sixteen, seventeen, eighteen, nineteen, twenty, twenty-one, twenty-two, twenty-three, twenty-four, twenty-five, twenty-six, twenty-seven, twenty-eight, twenty-nine, thirty, thirty-one, thirty-two, thirty-three, thirty-four, thirty-five, thirty-six, thirty-seven, thirty-eight, thirty-nine, forty, forty-one, forty-two, forty-three, forty-four, forty-five, forty-six, forty-seven, forty-eight, forty-nine, fifty, fifty-one, fifty-two, fifty-three, fifty-four, fifty-five, fifty-six, fifty-seven, fifty-eight, fifty-nine, sixty** wake up, go to school, go home, do your homework, take a bath, go to bed / usually	
3-2	アイスクリームコーン My favorite ice cream cone	●既習語　whichの練習 ●アイスクリームフレイバーの語彙	■Which ice cream cone do you want? ■Which size do you want? ■Triple, please.	**single, double, triple, mint, vanilla, chocolate, lemon, mango, coffee, strawberry**	
3-3	英語の音（フォニックス） Sounds of the Alphabet	●three-letter words ●短母音　a, e, i, o, u	■What's that? ■It is a	**cat, hat, bat** / **jet, net, pet** / **fin, pin, chin** / **hop, top, mop** / **sun, bun, gun** pat, rat, sat, mat, fat / wet, vet, met, pet, get / bit, fit, hit, mit, sit / cot, dot, hot, lot, not / cut, nut, but, gut, hut	three-letter words train
4-1	好きな教科 My favorite subject	●一般動詞疑問文　have like	■What do you have today? ■Do you like ...? ■Yes, I do. / No, I don't.	**math, English, science, P.E., social studies, Japanese, music, arts and crafts**	
4-2	ペットをかっていますか？ I want a big black dog.	●一般動詞疑問文　have want	■Do you have (want) ...? ■Yes, I do. / No, I don't.	**hamster, turtle, goldfish, lizard, beetle, rabbit, parrot, squirrel, frog** a head, ears, legs, a body, a tail	
4-3	英語を読んでみよう（フォニックス） Map or Mop?	●短母音　a, e, i, o, u ●three-letter words	■C, a, p, cap. ■Do you have a map or mop?	**map, cap, cup, pen, pin, mop, nut, net, fin, pot, pet, jet**	three-letter words story A fat bat ①
5-1	ぼくの家 My house	●疑問詞　where, whatで始まる疑問文 ●家の部屋の語彙	■Where are you? ■I am in the kitchen. ■What are you doing? ■I am cooking.	**kitchen, living room, bedroom, dining room, bathroom, garden, garage** writing a letter, washing, cleaning (vacuuming), eating, watching TV, reading a book / come, help, Dad	

5-2	サラダを作ってみよう Let's make a salad.	●野菜の語彙 ●既習語 have, likeの練習 ●How many …?	■I have …. ■I like … in my salad. ■How many … in the basket?	**lettuce, broccoli, cucumber, carrot, onion, green pepper, cabbage, corn, spinach, mushroom** / tomato, potato, apple toss, mix, delicious, We can tell!	
5-3	バランスのある食事 Food pyramid	●既習語 wantの練習 ●栄養グループの語彙 ●食べ物、飲み物の語彙	■Do you want …? ■What do you want? ■I want ….	**fried chicken, beef steak, roast pork, baked fish, rice, spaghetti, a sandwich, a hot dog, cheese, yogurt, a big scoop of ice cream, a cup of coffee, a cup of tea** Milk Group, Meat & Fish Group, Vegetable Group, Fruit Group, Grain Group / oil, sugar / butter / egg, chicken, beef / eggplant, pumpkin / grapes, lemon / bread, cereal, cookie	story A fat bat ②
6-1	朝起きて学校に行くまで In the morning	●命令形、身近な動詞句	■Hurry up. ■Change your clothes.	**change your clothes, have your breakfast, pack your bag, brush your teeth, wash your face, dry your face, comb your hair, put on your socks, put on your shoes, get your bag,** wake up, wash my face, brush my teeth, comb my hair, change my clothes, eat my toast, pack my bag, go to school	
6-2	みんなで出かけよう Let's go on a picnic.	●疑問詞 where, when, howで始まる疑問文 ●場所を表す句、時を表す句、手段を表す句とその順序 ●Shall we …?	■Where shall we go? ■When shall we go? ■How shall we go? ■That sounds great.	**park, school, airport, library, hospital, supermarket, train station, zoo** **to** the zoo / the airport / school / the hospital / the park / the supermarket / the library / the train station / Hawaii / Canada // **by** rocket / airplane / bus / train / balloon / ship, on foot // **on** April 17th, in April, on Wednesday, at 6 o'clock, in winter, at night, in the morning	
6-3	ほうかご、ねるまで In the evening	●命令形、身近な動詞句	■Hurry up. ■Do your homework.	**set the table, eat supper, do your homework, take a bath, wash your hair, dry your body, wash the dishes, dry the dishes, watch TV, put on pajamas** before, after (WORKBOOK)	story A red bug ①
7-1	せかいの天気 World weather forecast	●天候を表す形容詞 ●四季の語彙	■How is the weather in Canada? ■It is sunny and hot.	**spring, summer, fall, winter, hot, warm, cool, cold, fine** cloudy, sunny, rainy, windy, snowy, humid, weather report	
7-2	つくえの上の本は何色？ What color is the book on the desk?	●前置詞	■Where is the blue book? ■It's on the desk. ■What color is the book on the desk? ■It's blue.	**on, in, under, by, over, between** on the desk, in the desk, under the desk, by the desk, over the desk, between the desks	
7-3	わたしの持ち物 What do you have in your bag?	●加算名詞の複数形 ●文房具、身の回りの物の語彙	■What do you have in your bag? ■Show me what you have.	**tissue(s), handkerchief, key, cell phone, game, comic book, CD, scissors, glue stick, marker(s), pencil sharpener, sticker(s), snack(s), water bottle** textbook, notebook, eraser / a book, books, no books / a pencil, pencils, no pencils	story A red bug ②
8-1	助けてください！ Will you help me?	●ていねいな命令形とていねいなお願いの仕方 ●…, please. ●Will you …? ●TPR	■Will you show me your notebook, please? ■Show me your notebook, please. ■Show me your notebook.	**open the window, leave the window open, close the window, turn on the light, open the door, leave the door open, close the door, turn off the light** ladder / Watch your step!	
8-2	なんてすてきな先生でしょう What a nice teacher!	●感嘆文 ●形容詞	■What a nice teacher! ■What a short pencil!	**strong, weak, tall, short, fat, thin, clean, dirty, young, old, scary** pretty, big, little, long, short	
8-3	いっしょに遊んでもいいですか？ May I join you?	●助動詞 may ●副詞 up, down, right, left	■May I join you? ■Yes, you may. / No, you may not.	**play the game, play the CD, use the computer, use a dictionary, come in, go out, speak Japanese** / up, down, left, right	story A red bug ③
9-1	みんなのいけん Various opinions	●一般動詞 三人称単数現在のs ●live(s)とlike(s)を使った肯定文	■Yumi likes …. ■He likes swimming.	**tennis, judo, skiing, dodgeball, soccer, basketball, table tennis, baseball, volleyball** swimming	
9-2	たん生日 My birthday	●12か月、日付、序数 ●三人称単数現在のs, has ●whoが主語になる疑問文	■Who has a birthday in January? ■I have my birthday in January. ■Yumi has her birthday in January.	**first, second, third, fourth, fifth, sixth, seventh, eighth, ninth, tenth, eleventh, twelfth, thirteenth, fourteenth, fifteenth, sixteenth, seventeenth, eighteenth, nineteenth, twentieth, twenty-first, twenty-second, twenty-third, twenty-fourth, twenty-fifth, twenty-sixth, twenty-seventh, twenty-eighth, twenty-ninth, thirtieth, thirty-first** / in front of, behind	ch, sh, th
9-3	しょうらいのしょくぎょう We are twenty five years old.	●職業の語彙 ●職業をたずねる	■What do you do? ■I am a florist. ■Mark is a cook.	**cook, teacher, dentist, florist, scientist, nurse, soccer player, baker, cartoonist, cabin attendant**	
10-1	ストーリー An Elephant is Walking	●総復習 （現在進行形, 三単現s, canなど）		skate, swim, ski, sing / find, take, say, half / Let's share it!	
10-2	ストーリー In a Cabin in the Woods	●総復習		hat, shirt, pants, shoes, belt, scarf, bag / knock, shoot, hide, come inside / safe, dead	
10-3	友達とわたし My friend and me	●総復習（自己紹介と友達の紹介）	■I want to be a teacher. ■He wants to be a cook.		

1 one	2 two	3 three	4 four	5 five	6 six	7 seven	8 eight	9 nine	10 ten
11 eleven	12 twelve	13 thirteen	14 fourteen	15 fifteen	16 sixteen	17 seventeen	18 eighteen	19 nineteen	20 twenty
21 twenty-one	22 twenty-two	23 twenty-three	24 twenty-four	25 twenty-five	26 twenty-six	27 twenty-seven	28 twenty-eight	29 twenty-nine	30 thirty
31 thirty-one	32 thrity-two	33 thirty-three	34 thirty-four	35 thirty-five	36 thirty-six	37 thirty-seven	38 thirty-eight	39 thirty-nine	40 forty
41 forty-one	42 forty-two	43 forty-three	44 forty-four	45 forty-five	46 forty-six	47 forty-seven	48 forty-eight	49 forty-nine	50 fifty
51 fifty-one	52 fifty-two	53 fifty-three	54 fifty-four	55 fifty-five	56 fifty-six	57 fifty-seven	58 fifty-eight	59 fifty-nine	60 sixty
61 sixty-one	62 sixty-two	63 sixty-three	64 sixty-four	65 sixty-five	66 sixty-six	67 sixty-seven	68 sixty-eight	69 sixty-nine	70 seventy
71 seventy-one	72 seventy-two	73 seventy-three	74 seventy-four	75 seventy-five	76 seventy-six	77 seventy-seven	78 seventy-eight	79 seventy-nine	80 eighty
81 eighty-one	82 eighty-two	83 eighty-three	84 eighty-four	85 eighty-five	86 eighty-six	87 eighty-seven	88 eighty-eight	89 eighty-nine	90 ninety
91 ninety-one	92 ninety-two	93 ninety-three	94 ninety-four	95 ninety-five	96 ninety-six	97 ninety-seven	98 ninety-eight	99 ninety-nine	100 one hundred

My name is

PROGRESS REPORT

4	6	8	10	12	14	16	18	20	22
24	26	28	30	32	34	36	38	40	42
44	46	48	50	52	54	56	58	60	62

☆ Challenge Chart ☆

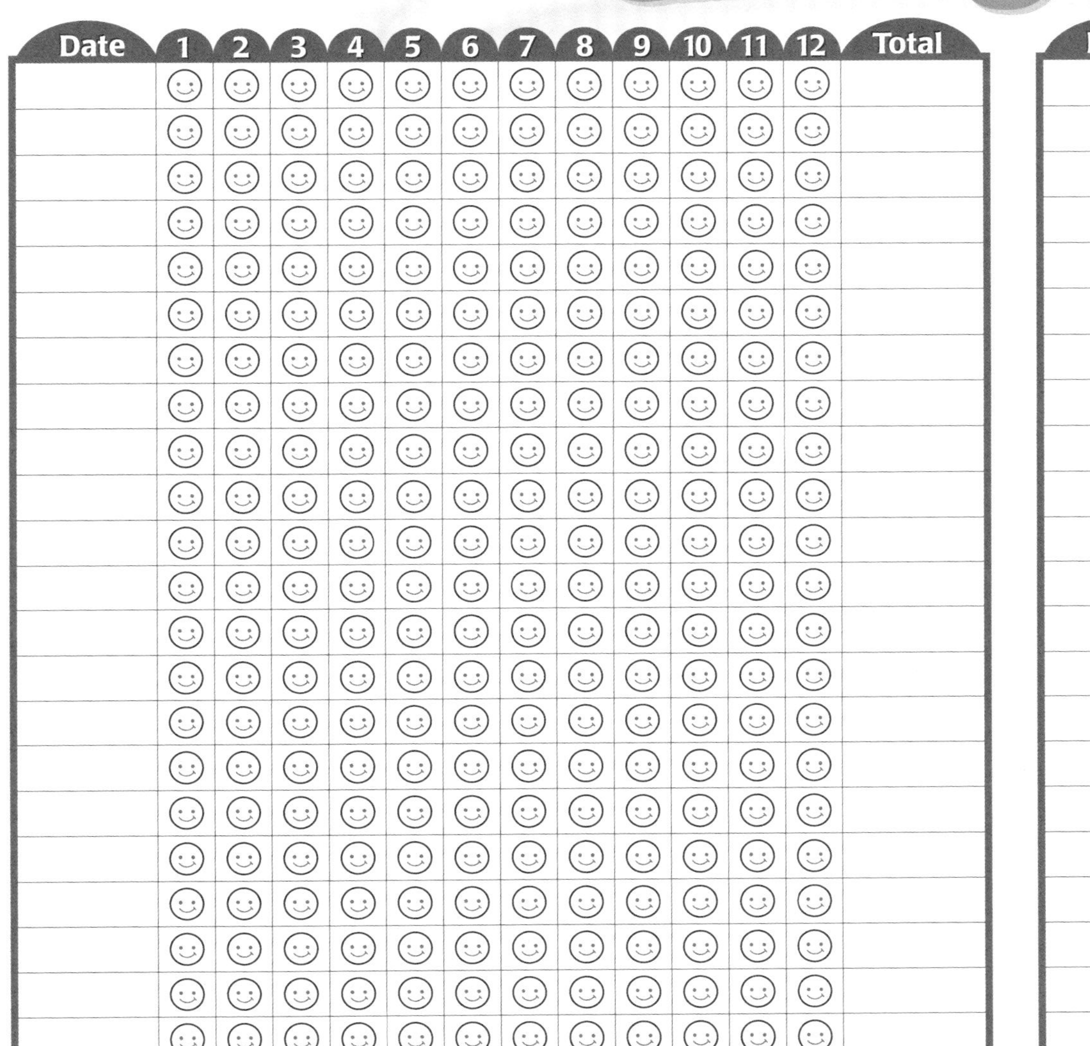

Date	1	2	3	4	5	6	7	8	9	10	11	12	Total
	☺	☺	☺	☺	☺	☺	☺	☺	☺	☺	☺	☺	
	☺	☺	☺	☺	☺	☺	☺	☺	☺	☺	☺	☺	
	☺	☺	☺	☺	☺	☺	☺	☺	☺	☺	☺	☺	
	☺	☺	☺	☺	☺	☺	☺	☺	☺	☺	☺	☺	
	☺	☺	☺	☺	☺	☺	☺	☺	☺	☺	☺	☺	
	☺	☺	☺	☺	☺	☺	☺	☺	☺	☺	☺	☺	
	☺	☺	☺	☺	☺	☺	☺	☺	☺	☺	☺	☺	
	☺	☺	☺	☺	☺	☺	☺	☺	☺	☺	☺	☺	
	☺	☺	☺	☺	☺	☺	☺	☺	☺	☺	☺	☺	
	☺	☺	☺	☺	☺	☺	☺	☺	☺	☺	☺	☺	
	☺	☺	☺	☺	☺	☺	☺	☺	☺	☺	☺	☺	
	☺	☺	☺	☺	☺	☺	☺	☺	☺	☺	☺	☺	
	☺	☺	☺	☺	☺	☺	☺	☺	☺	☺	☺	☺	
	☺	☺	☺	☺	☺	☺	☺	☺	☺	☺	☺	☺	
	☺	☺	☺	☺	☺	☺	☺	☺	☺	☺	☺	☺	
	☺	☺	☺	☺	☺	☺	☺	☺	☺	☺	☺	☺	
	☺	☺	☺	☺	☺	☺	☺	☺	☺	☺	☺	☺	
	☺	☺	☺	☺	☺	☺	☺	☺	☺	☺	☺	☺	
	☺	☺	☺	☺	☺	☺	☺	☺	☺	☺	☺	☺	
	☺	☺	☺	☺	☺	☺	☺	☺	☺	☺	☺	☺	
	☺	☺	☺	☺	☺	☺	☺	☺	☺	☺	☺	☺	
	☺	☺	☺	☺	☺	☺	☺	☺	☺	☺	☺	☺	

Date	1	2	3	4	5	6	7	8	9	10	11	12	Total
	☺	☺	☺	☺	☺	☺	☺	☺	☺	☺	☺	☺	
	☺	☺	☺	☺	☺	☺	☺	☺	☺	☺	☺	☺	
	☺	☺	☺	☺	☺	☺	☺	☺	☺	☺	☺	☺	
	☺	☺	☺	☺	☺	☺	☺	☺	☺	☺	☺	☺	
	☺	☺	☺	☺	☺	☺	☺	☺	☺	☺	☺	☺	
	☺	☺	☺	☺	☺	☺	☺	☺	☺	☺	☺	☺	
	☺	☺	☺	☺	☺	☺	☺	☺	☺	☺	☺	☺	
	☺	☺	☺	☺	☺	☺	☺	☺	☺	☺	☺	☺	
	☺	☺	☺	☺	☺	☺	☺	☺	☺	☺	☺	☺	
	☺	☺	☺	☺	☺	☺	☺	☺	☺	☺	☺	☺	
	☺	☺	☺	☺	☺	☺	☺	☺	☺	☺	☺	☺	
	☺	☺	☺	☺	☺	☺	☺	☺	☺	☺	☺	☺	
	☺	☺	☺	☺	☺	☺	☺	☺	☺	☺	☺	☺	
	☺	☺	☺	☺	☺	☺	☺	☺	☺	☺	☺	☺	
	☺	☺	☺	☺	☺	☺	☺	☺	☺	☺	☺	☺	
	☺	☺	☺	☺	☺	☺	☺	☺	☺	☺	☺	☺	
	☺	☺	☺	☺	☺	☺	☺	☺	☺	☺	☺	☺	
	☺	☺	☺	☺	☺	☺	☺	☺	☺	☺	☺	☺	
	☺	☺	☺	☺	☺	☺	☺	☺	☺	☺	☺	☺	
	☺	☺	☺	☺	☺	☺	☺	☺	☺	☺	☺	☺	
	☺	☺	☺	☺	☺	☺	☺	☺	☺	☺	☺	☺	
	☺	☺	☺	☺	☺	☺	☺	☺	☺	☺	☺	☺	

先生の質問にこたえて色をぬりましょう。

Students color in one happy face at a time on answering each of the teacher's questions during warm up/review time.

Certificate of Achievement

Awarded to ______________________

this __________ *day of* __________ , ________

for your great effort in

Learning World BOOK 2

Signed